I WANT TO BE A
CHIEF
MEDICAL
OFFICER
NOW WHAT

?

Rex Hoffman, MD, MBA, FACHE, CPE

CO-EDITOR: **Doug Koekkoek, MD**
CO-EDITOR: **Mark Olszyk, MD, MBA, CPE**
FOREWORD: **Peter Angood, MD**

American Association for
**PHYSICIAN
LEADERSHIP**

Published by **American Association for Physician Leadership, Inc.**
PO Box 96503 | BMB 97493 | Washington, DC 20090-6503

Website: www.physicianleaders.org

AAPL books are available at special quantity discounts to use as premiums and sales
promotions, or for use in corporate training programs. For more information, please write to
Special Sales at journal@physicianleaders.org

This publication is designed to provide general information and is sold with the
understanding that neither the author nor the publisher is engaged in rendering legal,
accounting, ethical, or clinical advice. If legal or other expert advice is required, the services
of a competent professional person should be sought.

13   8 7 6 5 4 3 2 1

Copyedited, typeset, indexed, and printed in the United States of America

PUBLISHER
Nancy Collins

PRODUCTION MANAGER
Jennifer Weiss

DESIGN & LAYOUT
Carter Publishing Studio

COPYEDITOR
Patricia George

*To dear old Dad, Dr. Richard B. Hoffman (1937–2011),
who was and continues to be my inspiration for becoming
a physician and chief medical officer.*

Acknowledgments

BRINGING THIS BOOK AND ITS AUTHORS together has been a real joy, not just for me, but for the others involved as well. On more than one occasion, I heard from an author that being able to offer advice to physicians aspiring to be chief medical officers was more fun than work.

Early on, I knew that I could not write this book on my own, so I recruited two co-editors, Doug Koekkoek and Mark Olszyk.

I met Doug during his days at Providence Health System, where he served as the chief medical officer of the Providence Medical Group. At that time, we collaborated on creating the *Providence Chief Medical Officer Handbook* that to this day is handed to new chief medical officers as they join Providence to help ease their way into the organization.

Today, Doug serves as the chief physician executive at Peace Health and, through his connections, was able to secure several of the authors in this book.

I had the pleasure of working with my other co-editor, Mark Olszyk, when we created *The Chief Medical Officer's Essential Handbook,* which was published by AAPL in 2023. Mark has a wealth of experience as a chief medical officer which was on full display in the numerous chapters he wrote in the handbook. During that project, we interacted with several chief medical officers who, fortunately for us, agreed to assist us with this book as well.

By partnering together, the three of us were able to identify and convince nine other authors to join this endeavor; the 12 of us bring you this book.

Another individual who has been very instrumental in making this book a reality is Nancy Collins from the American Association for Physician Leadership. Without her guidance and support, this book would have never gotten off the ground. For that reason, we will be eternally grateful to her.

Last, but certainly not least, a special shout out needs to go to the numerous physicians, patients, colleagues, and fellow chief medical officers each of us has had the pleasure of working with during our careers. In some way, each of these individuals has made us who we are today and shaped the way we approach and advise in different situations.

Table of Contents

About the Editor

DR. REX HOFFMAN KNEW HE WANTED TO BE A DOCTOR when he was in high school. He clearly remembers always being glued to his seat at the dinner table when his father, a physician, would come home and share stories about his day at the hospital. These stories were so captivating that not only did Hoffman end up going to medical school, but two years later, his sister did as well.

His journey in medicine started at Tulane School of Medicine, followed by a transitional year at Good Samaritan Hospital in Phoenix, Arizona, and, ultimately, a radiation oncology residency at the University of California, San Francisco.

Coming out of residency, he was recruited to Providence Saint Joseph's Medical Center in Burbank, California, where he worked as a radiation oncologist from 2001 to 2019, the last 11 ½ years as medical director. During this time, he served on many medical staff committees, including the Medical Executive Committee, the Credentials Committee, and the Utilization Management Committee.

In 2016–2018 Rex pursued a Business of Medicine MBA degree at Indiana University Kelley School of Business.

Shortly thereafter, in 2019, Hoffman became the chief medical officer at Providence Holy Cross Medical Center. In this role, he has led two Providence-wide initiatives: creating a Medical Directorship Playbook, which guided his fellow CMOs in managing medical directorships, and serving as the chief editor of a *Chief Medical Officer Handbook* designed to onboard new Providence CMOs.

From June 2020 through March 2022, he served as the chief medical officer for Providence's eight clinical institutes in Southern California: Cancer, Cardiovascular, Digestive Health, Mental Health, Neurosciences, Orthopedics, Research, and Women's and Children's.

In April 2022, he transitioned out of the clinical institute work and became the executive director of operations at Providence Holy Cross Medical Center, in addition to being the CMO.

In 2023, he collaborated with co-editor Erin Dupree and chief editor Mark Olszyk in producing *The Chief Medical Officer's Essential Handbook*. He co-authored the chapter on "Managing Contracts" and the commentary on "The CEO and the CMO" and "The CMO and the Chief Nursing Officer: Creating Synergy" chapters.

Outside of work, Hoffman enjoys spending time with his wife and two children, ages 5 and 7. His hobbies include wine tasting, hiking, and taking in a Los Angeles Clippers NBA basketball game.

Rex Hoffman, MD
Email: RexHoffmanMD@gmail.com

Foreword

By Peter Angood, MD, FRCS(C), FACS, MCCM, FAAPL(Hon)

I HAZARD A GUESS that many physicians have heard this:
You seem to be well-liked by your patients...
Other physicians seem to respect you...
Our staff seem to enjoy working with you, and...
Your outcomes compared to others seem terrific, so...
Congratulations, we want you to be the next Chief Medical Officer here!
Although a majority of these potential chief medical officers who hear this may not have any level of relevant leadership experience, they are still initially attracted to the job invitation and become curious about this choice for a career path.

This is a position not to be taken lightly in the current era of our healthcare industry.

The chief medical officer (CMO) role has been around in some fashion for a good number of years, but its importance and relevance rapidly escalated recently. The COVID pandemic certainly increased awareness of the significance of the CMO role, and for many healthcare delivery systems, the role has evolved to be one of critical importance and influence within administrative circles. At times, the scope of related responsibilities may even seem to be outsized for the role.

For those interested in pursuing the CMO role, this book offers an excellent approach to answer that core question of "Now what?" The book is laid out in such a fashion that you, the reader, will often feel as if the authors are sitting beside you, anticipating your thoughts and questions.

The book succeeds in this fashion because the authors are all veteran CMOs themselves and have experienced the many aspects — positive and negative —of the CMO role. They know the territory exceedingly well and are committed to helping you navigate this journey by answering your questions based on their direct experience. The overall layout and sequencing of the topics further reinforce the value and readability of the book.

The host and variety of issues, strategies, tactics, and problems for a CMO role in any organization can often seem daunting for the uninitiated, but the converse is also quite true. The necessary trend to consolidate true patient-centered care, the inevitable progress to value-based care models, the importance of improving workforce wellness, the ability to contribute to the improvement of quality, safety and efficiency initiatives, as well as the opportunity for being the interface professional with non-clinical administrators, to name just a few, can be exhilarating and deeply satisfying for those in CMO roles. Don't be daunted, be encouraged.

It is one thing to recognize the importance and the potential opportunity of becoming a CMO; it is quite a different matter to know how to obtain this role in the first place. This book is an excellent guide on the nuances of becoming a CMO and provides brilliant insights about the variety of issues at play while pursuing your first (or even second and third) CMO opportunity.

The book represents a well-written treatise on how to identify your potential for being a CMO and it helps you move through a host of resources and explore a variety of factors while making the final decision about becoming a CMO. This final choice is yours — do you want this job, and can you do it well?

At some level, all physicians are leaders, regardless of whether or not they are in formally titled roles. Yes, a variety of other new leadership roles are coming into place within healthcare, such as chief quality officer, chief medical informatics officer, and chief wellness officer. However, the CMO role offers the broadest and deepest set of opportunities within any organization or clinical delivery system.

The CMO role also offers high levels of personal satisfaction as a result of helping other physicians achieve their own leadership potential for professional growth and development.

Helping one's peers is a distinct privilege and a truly unique opportunity. Often, the CMO role involves varying levels of mentorship and coaching for other physicians. This rolls over to other clinical professionals, as well as many non-clinical administrators in an organization. As a result, the CMO role is high-profile and has a high impact on several levels. The net effect is markedly improved patient care processes coupled with improved patient care outcomes.

Interestingly, a July 2022 McKinsey analysis identified three primary CMO archetypes for consumer-facing companies beyond healthcare:

the policymaker and culture carrier, the guardian of the patient and the consumer, and the growth strategist. This represents another potential pathway for those considering CMO roles. The net effect is to help these consumer-facing organizations better interface with their customer base and improve their product lines.

The healthcare industry is exceedingly complex and will remain so for the foreseeable future. The CMO role is likely to become even more pivotal to developing successful transformations of clinical delivery systems — transformations that will ultimately improve the professional satisfaction of the workforce and the baseline health of our patients.

Regardless of how one approaches this book and for what potential endpoint, the information provided in the book on how to become a CMO in the current healthcare marketplace is a must-read. This should also be a serious read for those who are involved with preparing or hiring individuals for CMO roles.

Enjoy your read. The outcome will be greater success in becoming a CMO and improved professional satisfaction.

Preface

Rex Hoffman, MD, MBA, FACHE, CPE

FIVE AND A HALF YEARS AGO, I was a radiation oncologist who had been in practice for 18 years, was a medical director, had served on virtually every committee in the hospital, was on the foundation board, and had chaired the cancer committee for 10 years. But, after reflecting on my career, I decided I wanted to become a chief medical officer. ... So now what? Where do I start?

I had many questions, but depending on who I spoke with, I got different answers. Did I need to be a chief of staff first? Was it essential to get an MBA or MHA? Was there value in becoming a Certified Physician Executive (CPE)?

How do I create a resume that will make me an attractive candidate for a CMO position? Heck, how do I even find out where a CMO position is open? When I do, what should I look for in the job description? What should I ask when trying to decide if I even want to apply?

Then, if I am fortunate enough to be offered an interview, what should I ask, be prepared to answer, or look for in the person interviewing me?

These and many other questions were on my mind, and there was no single source to go to for the answers. Thus, my objective in this book is to help you answer these questions and more.

Recognizing that not all of the people you ask these questions will agree, our strategy for this book was to query multiple people in positions that regularly hire CMOs: chief executive officers and regional and system CMOs. Altogether, we interviewed 10 chief executives, two regional chief medical officers, and three system CMOs. They came from different hospitals, health systems, and states. We asked each one a list of questions — those I posed earlier as well as some others. The themes we gleaned from their responses are shared in these pages.

Finding a CMO job can be like searching for a needle in the haystack, particularly if you do not know where to look. We will give you some ideas on where to seek out such jobs. In addition, once you find a CMO job that looks like it has potential, how do you decipher if it is the right fit for you?

We'll share some tips and tricks on what to look for when reviewing a job description.

We also include a section on résumé writing so you can put your best foot forward when looking to land a CMO job in a hospital, medical group, or health plan. Your résumé should make you an attractive candidate to recruiters and others you are likely to encounter in the job search process.

Interviewing for a CMO role can be stressful. To prepare you for this important aspect of the journey, we have crafted a chapter that examines all components of an interview, including what to wear, how to prepare, and what to ask at the end to give you the best chance of performing well and separating yourself from the competition.

Chief medical officers don't exist only in hospitals; there are CMOs of medical groups, health plans, and health systems. Consequently, subject matter experts in each of these areas share their insights and experiences to help those aspiring to one of these roles.

Assisting me in this undertaking is Dr. Doug Koekkoek, who was previously the CMO of Providence's system-wide medical group and now is the chief physician executive (or system CMO) of Peace Health System, and Dr. Mark Olszyk, chief medical officer at Carroll Hospital in Maryland for 10 years and chief editor of *The Chief Medical Officer's Essential Guidebook*. Together, we bring a wealth of experience and connections to this topic.

In essence, this book will provide you with a guide and some recommendations as you seek to become a first-time CMO or are looking for that second CMO job. I wish I had such a blueprint to help me when I set out to become a CMO. I am excited for you! Let's get started.

PART I

Want to be a CMO?

The Chief Medical Officer Role

Rex Hoffman, MD, MBA, FACHE, CPE

S O, YOU WANT TO BE a chief medical officer? Well, you have taken the first important step and opened this book, which was written to help you on your journey to becoming a chief medical officer (CMO). Each of the important steps necessary to achieve this goal is outlined in the chapters ahead.

Before providing an overview of what you are about to embark on, let me share with you my personal journey from practicing physician to CMO.

MY CMO JOURNEY

The year was 2017. I had been a radiation oncologist for 17 years, during which I had designed a radiation oncology department, been a medical director, chaired the Cancer Committee, and led Providence Health System's Cancer Institute. I was at a point in my career when I felt I had accomplished as much as I had set out to as a radiation oncologist. I was ready to tackle the next project but did not know what it was.

At the time, I was attending Indiana Kelley School of Business and had set my sights on obtaining a Business of Medicine degree. In my class was a colleague who was a chief medical officer at a hospital. Back then, I was not very familiar with what a CMO did, since I rarely interacted with my CMO. So, I asked him what a typical day was like for him.

When I heard about his daily activities, I became glued to our conversations. In fact, each month when I returned to Indiana for a session, I sought him out to hear about his latest escapades. Whether designing a strategy for his hospital or working to improve physician engagement, it all interested me.

By early 2018, I knew that I wanted to be a chief medical officer, but I wasn't sure how to go about it. Since I was part of a large health system, the first thing I did was reach out to several CMOs I had interacted with in some system-wide initiatives. Interestingly, each one had a different experience. Nevertheless, I was convinced that this was what I wanted to do for the next phase of my career.

In addition to chief medical officers, I reached out to a few chief executives, since they were the ones who hired chief medical officers, and asked them to please let me know when a CMO position became available. I also contacted the regional chief medical officer and health system chief medical officer to let them know I was looking to become a CMO.

So, the word was out there.

The large health system in which I worked spans seven states, and at that time, all the CMO positions in my area were filled. Therefore, when asked if I was "willing to relocate," I said that I was.

In late 2018, I got lucky. A CMO position became available at a hospital in my health system that was only 20 miles from my home. I had identified the target and now needed to prepare for the application process.

Another stroke of luck was that I had previously met the chief executive officer of this hospital and respected him. He had a fantastic reputation among those with whom he worked, which was important to me. I applied for the position and was invited to come in for an interview.

To prepare for the interview, I queried several of the chief medical officers I had previously connected with to get a sense as to what types of questions I would be asked; I then practiced my responses. I also spent a lot of time going over the job description, which prompted some great questions for me to ask.

The day of the interview arrived. I recall two separate group interviews: one interview with members of the medical staff and a second interview with the executive leadership team at the hospital. I had never been so glad that I had thoroughly researched the hospital, its medical staff, and its job description, and then practiced my responses. None of the interviewers' questions caught me by surprise.

I cannot stress enough the importance of patience during this process. Because you likely are not the only candidate for such a prestigious position, you may need to wait for a few weeks to hear your fate, which is what I did. When the call came from the chief executive officer that the job was mine, I was elated.

ANATOMY OF THE BOOK

Physicians often ask me to what I attribute my success in becoming a chief medical officer. My answer is multi-faceted: being inquisitive, doing the necessary research, and being prepared for each step of the process. The goal of this book is to help you with these different facets so you, too, can get the coveted chief medical officer job you are seeking.

This book is divided into four parts; each focuses on a separate aspect of the "I want to be a CMO" journey. Part I reviews what a chief medical officer does so there are no misconceptions about this role. In addition, determining when to leave one's clinical practice to become a chief medical officer can be very stressful and demands much thought and reflection. Doug Koekkoek shares his journey, as well as others he has witnessed over the years. He also discusses the pros and cons of maintaining a clinical practice while being a chief medical officer.

Part II was informed by the feedback we received from the surveys as well as some commentary by the respective authors of these chapters to give you an idea about the importance of having experience or an MBA/MHA/MMM/CPE or fellowship when applying for a chief medical officer role. And if there is a benefit to obtaining these degrees, how does one go about it?

These survey results also shed light on what key attributes those who hire CMOs are looking for so you can self-reflect and determine if you have these attributes or plan how you can get them to set yourself up for success during the application process.

Part III focuses on the application process itself. We'll begin with strategies to find a CMO job: where to look, who to talk to, and where to go. Michele Arnold shares her experiences and provides some recommendations.

Next, Steve Brass discusses how he assesses a specific CMO job and what to look out for when reviewing job descriptions. Gary Foster, a certified resume writer, offers a chapter on writing your resume to put your best foot forward when looking to land a chief medical officer job in a hospital, medical group, health plan, or regional/system role in a health system. We want your resume to make you an attractive candidate to recruiters and others you are likely to encounter in the job search process.

Interviewing for a CMO position can be stressful. To prepare you for this important aspect of the journey, Mark Olszyk contributes a chapter that looks at all components of an interview, including what to wear, how to prepare, and what to ask at the end to give you the best chance of performing well and separating yourself from the competition. He shares the dos and don'ts from his firsthand experience.

Part IV offers advice from four individuals who have held different CMO roles over the course of their careers. Reka Danko discusses what it is like being a CMO at a hospital; Christopher Hall shares how the role is slightly different if you are the CMO of a medical group. Next, Mike Menen discusses what it is like being a CMO of a health plan. This section is rounded out by Amy Compton Phillips, who shares what it is like to be the CMO of a health system. Each of these CMOs' experiences will illustrate how varied CMO jobs can be.

After reading Parts I-IV, hopefully you have set out on your journey to be a CMO and landed the CMO job you desire. If so, Part V was created for you.

In this section, Dr. Koekkoek suggests how you should spend your first 90 days on the job. This initial period has been shown to significantly impact whether you will be a successful CMO, so it is worth paying attention to. Also in Part V, Gabriella Sherman shares the importance of having a mentor in your journey to become a CMO, as well as giving back as a mentor once in the role.

Each CMO got into their role through a different route. When pursuing such a job, why not separate yourself from the competition! Reading this book will help you get there.

It has been said that "luck is when preparation meets opportunity." The "pearls of wisdom" in the chapters ahead will help you prepare for and seek opportunities. So good luck!

CHAPTER 1

What Is a Chief Medical Officer?

Rex Hoffman, MD, MBA, FACHE, CPE

I T DEPENDS....

The title of chief medical officer (CMO) is used in many countries to identify the senior government official designated as head of medical services, sometimes at the national level. The post is held by a physician who advises and leads a team of medical experts on matters of public health importance.[1] In the United States, this senior government official is referred to as the surgeon general; in Canada, the title is chief public health officer.[2]

Alternatively, *Becker's Hospital Review* describes the chief medical officer as a senior executive acting as a liaison between physicians and hospital executives. This individual oversees the quality of care at the hospital and manages the hiring, training, and performance evaluation of physicians on staff.[2]

A wide variety of organizations have chief medical officers, including Disney, Constellation Brands, and the Mayo Clinic; however, their role as the professional lead of all physicians at a hospital, in a medical group, in a health plan, or in a health system is the focus of this book.

Two other roles are similar to the role of the CMO: vice president of medical affairs and chief clinical officer.

Vice President of Medical Affairs. The title vice president of medical affairs (VPMA) is sometimes used interchangeably with chief medical officer, but the roles differ. Although most hospitals have either a CMO or a VPMA, some hospitals employ both, with each having distinct responsibilities. When both positions are present, the VPMA generally reports to the CMO.[3] The core distinction between the two positions is the level of strategic input the physician leader provides to their organization.[4]

Chief Clinical Officer. Another job title often used interchangeably with CMO is chief clinical officer (CCO) although, again, the roles differ. CCOs are primarily tasked with overseeing patient engagement and clinical quality outcomes. They often are the "systems thinkers" who prioritize lean system performance requirements to reduce waste and improve care quality. Depending on the organization, a CCO also may assist in medical staff development, clinical integration, and physician partnerships.[5]

THE ROLE OF THE CHIEF MEDICAL OFFICER

The role of the CMO has evolved over time. For many years, it was a part-time gig, often filled by a clinically retired senior physician and reflecting more of a VPMA role. In the 1980s, the role transitioned from coaching the novice chief of staff on physician discipline, to quality and safety, to areas like service line emergency department call coverage and contracting, to strategy, population management, and community engagement.

Chief medical officers can be full-time or part-time administrators. If part-time, the remainder of their workday may be spent practicing clinically. Some people believe that the chief medical officers who maintain a part-time clinical practice have more credibility with the medical staff since they, too, are in the trenches. This may have some merit; however, there is no doubt that working in both capacities may limit the CMO's ability to be successful in both roles. There are always exceptions, though, as I know some very successful part-time CMOs who also maintain a clinical practice. An argument can be made for the value of both scenarios.

It's often said that when you have talked to one chief medical officer about what they do, you have talked to ONE chief medical officer about what they do, as there is great variability in how a CMO spends their time. In most cases, the primary responsibilities of a chief medical officer, whether full-time or part-time, include focusing on quality assurance, risk management, compensation arrangements, case management, credentialing, performance review, and conflict resolution.

Quality Assurance

When it comes to quality assurance, hospital-acquired infections (HAIs) are front and center. The CMO must be seen leading the charge on minimizing

HAIs: CAUTIs (catheter-associated urinary tract infections), CLABSIs (central line-associated bloodstream infections), C. difficile, and SSIs (surgical site infections), plus focus on other metrics their organization is prioritizing.

In my organization, these other metrics include ensuring geriatric hip fractures get from the ER to OR within 24 hours, guaranteeing goals-of-care conversations take place for every patient who is in the intensive care unit for at least five days, achieving NTSV (nulliparous, term, singleton, and vertex) Caesarean section rates less than 23.6%, and decreasing sepsis mortality rate. Each organization has its own priorities.

Risk Management

Risk management entails dealing with any situation that puts the organization at risk. Areas where this may come into play include privacy, medical necessity, revenue cycle compliance, fraud and abuse, conflicts of interest, and unexpected patient harm. For example, patients trust their health information will be kept private; therefore, chief medical officers must educate physicians about the importance of protected health information (PHI) to avoid privacy breaches.

It is not medically necessary or appropriate to bill a higher level of service when a lower level of service is sufficient. Doing so can get the institution and the physician into trouble. Therefore, documenting in one's notes the medical necessity of a service to support the patient's condition and all the other elements that in your clinical judgment were relevant in determining the most appropriate treatment plan for the patient is critical. To avoid over-billing and to ensure a physician's documentation is accurate, chief medical officers often work closely with the clinical documentation and integrity team.

Another area that requires risk management is fraud and abuse. The chief medical officer must be well-versed in the Anti-Kickback Statute, the Physician Self-Referral Law, and the Federal False Claims Act. Because of their stature in the organization along with their connections to vendors, physicians are subject to having conflicts of interest. These occur when personal interests or activities influence or appear to influence actions or behaviors. Consequently, chief medical officers ensure the physicians they work with are well-versed in the verbiage and actions associated with conflicts of interest.

Unexpected events that cause patients harm can also put an organization at risk of being sued. Many organizations have employed the CANDOR (Communication and Optimal Resolution) process to respond in a timely, thorough, and just manner. Promptly disclosing the error to the patient and expressing remorse that preventable harm occurred has been shown to mitigate the risk to the organization and result in fewer lawsuits. The chief medical officer often plays a leading role at the time of disclosure.

Physician Compensation

Physician compensation is another area chief medical officers need to be well-versed in. Employment agreements, medical directorships, and professional service agreements (PSAs) are common today, and what one can and cannot do needs to be clearly understood and adhered to. Having a basic understanding of what FMV (fair market value) is will go a long way toward ensuring you are doing the right thing for your organization.

To ensure these agreements provide value to the organization, the CMO also plays an active role in creating performance and quality goals in each agreement and updates them regularly. These goals should stretch the physician but also be realistic.

When creating these agreements, the CMO must also be well-versed in some of the basics of healthcare law including such regulations as the Stark Law, Anti-Kickback Statute, and False Claims Act to ensure that they and the organization are being compliant and risk averse.

Case Management

Another important relationship for the CMO is with case management. The success of a CMO depends on how they fare with length of stay (LOS) and 30-day readmissions. Being actively involved with utilization management and working closely with physician advisors is essential.

The length of time a patient is in the hospital is important whether you are a CMO at a hospital, in a medical group, or part of a health plan. Achieving a good length of stay requires the chief medical officer and case management to focus on the time a patient spends in the hospital as well as their transition to a post-acute setting such as a skilled nursing facility (SNF), board and care, and long-term acute care (LTAC) facility.

Consequently, CMOs in my organization interact regularly with these partners to ensure a smooth transition from the hospital to one of these facilities. Case management personnel and I not only visit our partners quarterly, but we meet with their leaders monthly to ensure that we are aligned as much as possible in our objectives.

It is one thing to make sure patients don't stay in the hospital longer than they need to and another to make sure they don't bounce back after being discharged by being readmitted within 30 days. A CMO's priority should be monitoring and trying to avoid patients being readmitted within 30 days after being treated for acute myocardial infarction, post-coronary artery bypass graft, congestive heart failure, pneumonia, chronic obstructive pulmonary disease, and following total hip and knee surgery. Getting length of stay and readmissions right is important because both are associated with financial penalties if we perform poorly.

Credentialing

Medical staff credentialing, privileging, and internal compliance with policies and procedures are other areas the CMO needs to focus on. In this capacity, the CMO works closely with and oversees the medical staff office (MSO).

Credentialing is the process by which medical staff membership is conferred. The medical staff office is responsible for collecting and organizing all the data needed to adjudicate the files of applicants for primary appointment and reappointment. Privileging is the process of defining the scope of practice allowed to a clinician in the hospital or medical group.

The medical staff office maintains practice standards and assures the CMO that they are applied consistently. Whenever a change in privileging criteria is considered, or when a new privilege is established, the MSO does the necessary due diligence around standards and safety to guide the decisions of medical staff leaders and ensures compliance with the governing documents.

It is a privilege to be granted membership and privileges at a hospital, in a medical group, or in a health plan, and as such, the process needs to be taken very seriously. Although the medical staff office is responsible for ensuring the process is followed precisely, since the MSO is overseen by the chief medical officer, it is ultimately the CMO's responsibility to ensure things get done right. Getting credentialing and privileging right is essential to optimizing patient care and so must be prioritized. The organized medical staff must comply with its own policies and procedures; failure to do so puts the organization, hospital, and professional staff in legal, ethical, and financial jeopardy.

Performance Evaluation

Most physicians provide highly reliable high-quality care; however, some don't. It is for this reason that CMOs need to be involved with ongoing and focused peer performance evaluations to ensure appropriate, safe care is being provided.

Sometimes a physician may behave inappropriately by disrespecting another person in the organization. In such instances it is the CMO's job to address the issue(s) and resolve the conflict. There is often a code of conduct within an organization that all caregivers and physicians must abide by. When physicians do not, it triggers a disruptive physician policy that the CMO needs to be aware of to ensure everyone is treated respectfully.

To address such situations and mitigate the risk to the organization, chief medical officers must meet with and counsel the physician whose behavior is the matter at hand. This often involves resolving a conflict between the physician and someone else. At the end of the day, everyone deserves to be treated with respect and it is the responsibility of the CMO to ensure this when it comes to the physicians.

ADDITIONAL RESPONSIBILITIES

Other responsibilities often include participating in strategic planning, promoting physician wellness, attending medical staff meetings, working closely with other members of the C-suite, leading by influence, educating physicians on the importance of value-based care, overseeing crisis management, and being a mentor.

Strategic Planning

To ensure their organization has a bright future with growth, executives are involved with strategic planning. The CMO plays an important role in this capacity when it comes to optimizing various service lines, reviewing or approving new technology, and recruiting new physicians.

At Providence Holy Cross Medical Center, we have a very large lung cancer screening program with more than 600 patients being actively surveyed since many of their lesions are peripheral and have not been amenable to lung biopsies. When I was approached by two pulmonologists inquiring about whether we wanted to invest in an ION bronchoscopy program to safely biopsy many of these lesions, I got excited; however, because it required a significant investment, I needed to do my research. After learning more about this technology and how it could help many of our patients, we decided to bring this program to Mission Hills, California. Today we have seven pulmonologists and a thoracic surgeon committed to this program.

Physician Well-being

Growth is exciting, but with it often comes more work for the physicians. Sometimes such added work can affect their well-being. Unfortunately, over the past few years, the rate of physician burnout across the nation has gone up significantly, making this another important area for the chief medical officer's focus.

As an advocate for the physicians I represent, I constantly look for ways to assist them. In fact, when I am asked if I miss taking care of patients now that I am a chief medical officer, my response is "No, because the doctors I represent are now my patients." As such, I constantly explore ways to keep them healthy and successful.

From the time I first meet the physicians and throughout their time on the medical staff, I check on them, always looking for ways to set them up for success, both personally and professionally. A big part of this is making sure they have access to resources for their mental health if necessary.

At my institution, we have taken a several-pronged approach to wellness that includes creating a Physician Well-Being Leadership Council of 12 physicians from a variety of specialties who work closely to develop and implement strategies to promote physician well-being across the medical staff. They regularly review what other organizations, such as the Mayo Clinic, American Medical Association, and Stanford Medical, have implemented to determine if any of these approaches would benefit our medical staff.

Some items that we have come up with in the past year include a list of items nurses should not call doctors about between 11 p.m. and 6 a.m., and a single-page document that provides guidance on how to relax each day.

In addition, I work closely with the physician who chairs our physician well-being committee and regularly check in with physicians on my medical staff who show signs/symptoms of burnout or are prone to this condition. This has paid huge dividends when it comes to identifying physicians at risk and building relationships with the medical staff. Our provider engagement survey in 2022 revealed that these strategies appear to be working, since the rate of burnout at our medical center went down significantly compared to 2020 and the medical staff gave high marks to their relationship with the administration.

Teamwork

The chief medical officer is responsible for updating the medical staff on what is going on and representing administration in different facets of hospital operations.

To fulfill these roles, I attend daily medical staff meetings — sometimes up to five medical staff meetings in a single day. At these meetings, questions may arise about issues that are out of physicians' control, such as a process or policy that nursing or administration has put in place. It is essential for me as the CMO to attend these meetings as a representative of administration and as an advocate for the medical staff. This allows me to weigh in on issues and address any barriers physicians are encountering.

As members of the C-suite, chief medical officers work closely with the other executives on the team, such as chief executive officer, chief nursing officer, chief financial officer, chief human resources officer, and chief philanthropy officer, among others. As a chief medical officer, I have a unique relationship with each of these individuals.

The chief executive officer and I focus on strategy for the hospital, physician recruitment, program development, service line optimization, and physician contract negotiations. The chief nursing officer and I focus on optimizing the relationship between nurses and physicians when it comes to consistently delivering high-quality healthcare and obtaining good patient outcomes. Nurses and physicians often collaborate on quality metrics, minimizing hospital-acquired infections, and decreasing length of stay and 30-day readmissions.

With the chief financial officer, the CMO looks at costs and return on investment (ROI) when it comes to optimizing different service lines, such as purchasing new equipment or recruiting a physician. CMOs work with the chief human resources officer in unfortunate situations when there is a conflict between a member of the medical staff and a caregiver. The CMO works closely with the chief philanthropy officer to increase awareness among the medical staff when it comes to identifying grateful patients and potential donors.

Leading by Influence

Successful CMOs lead by influence as opposed to being manipulative or patronizing to accomplish the many roles and responsibilities they have. They work closely with the chief of staff and department chairs to navigate medical staff affairs. The goal is to create a culture in which the physicians feel supported while at the same time prioritizing high-quality care, performance improvement, and case management goals.

In their capacity as leaders and physician advocates, CMOs must be aware that others are always watching them, and if they want to be influential, they should always lead by example. By working together, the medical staff and CMO can make great strides toward achieving the organization's goals.

Professional Development

The past few years have seen an increased focus on value-based care or the delivery of high-quality care at a lower price. Consequently, there has been a shift in the ways medical groups and physicians are reimbursed from fee for service to this more value-based care approach. Chief medical officers must have a basic understanding of both models because, in many cases, it will be up to the CMOs to educate the physicians they work with on the nuances of each.

Crisis Management

During times of crisis, CMOs often find themselves in a leadership role, tasked with bringing together the medical staff and others, including nursing and ancillary services. This may be in the capacity of an incident commander during a natural disaster such as a fire or earthquake. During the recent COVID pandemic, many chief medical officers found themselves working closely with physicians on the medical staff, nurses, and local authorities to help their organizations navigate the vast amount of information that was coming at them from a multitude of directions. Throughout the pandemic, the CMO took on the role of master communicator, providing updates, education, and crisis alerts on issues such as masking mandates, vaccine mandates, and new therapeutics like Remdesivir and Ivermectin.

Pandemic aside, CMOs communicate with physicians on the medical staff, informing them of new regulations, new technology, shortages of drugs and supplies, and the constantly changing rules and regulations.

Mentoring

Most chief medical officers have had a mentor before coming into the role. Once in the role, it is important for the chief medical officer to give back and mentor physicians who aspire to get into administration or take on larger roles. In essence, CMOs are building the pipeline of future leaders.

As a hospital-based chief medical officer, I mentor four physicians, each of whom has a different goal. Not only am I giving back, but I also derive great joy from being able to help these physicians realize their goals.

THE IMPORTANCE OF RELATIONSHIPS

Although there are many roles and responsibilities in the life of a chief medical officer, the main barometer of success is whether they are good at building and maintaining relationships with the physicians in their organization.

Some of the approaches I have taken to build relationships include regularly eating and socializing in the doctor's dining room, meeting and greeting new physicians when they join the medical staff, and regularly attending medical staff functions both on and off-campus. It is amazing what can be accomplished when chief medical officers work side by side with those they represent.

Whether a chief medical officer works at a hospital, in a medical group, for a health plan, or for a health system, their responsibilities may extend beyond what has been discussed in this chapter. For more specific details related to each of these entities, I refer you to chapters 10–13 in this book.

REFERENCES

1. Nice A. Institute for Government. Chief Medical Officer. https://www.institutefor government.org.uk/article/explainer/chief-medical-officer

2. Wikipedia. Chief Medical Officer. 2023.

3. Olszyk MD (ed.) The Chief Medical Officer's Essential Guidebook. Washington, DC: American Association for Physician Leadership; 2023. page 4.

4. Dister L. CMO or VPMA – Is There a Difference? *Physician Executive*. 2009;35(3): 12–16.

5. Dyrda L. 38 Hospital and Health System C-level Roles, Defined. *Becker's Hospital Review*. June 13, 2017.

CHAPTER 2

Is It Time to Transition to a CMO Job?

Douglas A. Koekkoek, MD

T HE WORK OF A CMO is a substantial departure from full-time clinical work, so the decision to become a CMO is one that the wise physician leader takes a very measured and thoughtful approach to contemplating. The wrong timing in making this career pivot can sour the aspiring CMO on leadership work in such a way that they are lost forever to the administrative side of medicine and will never contribute to what might have been a long and impactful career guiding a hospital or medical group.

When considering whether the time is right to start on the CMO career path, think about the following questions.

DO I HAVE THE NECESSARY EXPERIENCE?

Most chief medical officers have a few gaps in their experience when they take on their first CMO job. Much like the "practice of medicine," you don't graduate medical school and residency having managed every possible ailment or injury; so, it is with your job as a CMO. You won't know everything, but there are some basic job functions that would be best learned before landing the job.

Personnel Management

Chief among these aspects is managing physician behavior and putting in place clinical performance improvement plans. If you haven't had a job where you were accountable to manage a colleague who was struggling clinically or behaviorally, then you probably aren't ready for your first CMO job. Fortunately, there are a multitude of ways to get this experience.

Department chair, member of the peer review committee, or medical director in charge of a clinic or service line are all positions in which you have accountability for the clinical quality and professional behavior of your peers and in which you are called upon to help a colleague who is "under-performing." In addition to practical experience learned in one of these roles, the aspiring CMO should take part in formal didactic training in managing performance and behavior.

Taking a course in crucial conversations or similar structured courses is a nice complement to on-the-job training. Watching and learning from a more senior physician leader is an even better path. "See one, do one, teach one" is not just for clinical procedures — it's a fine way to learn how to manage the performance of clinicians.

Medical Staff Affairs

If it is a hospital CMO role you aspire to, a strong background in medical staff affairs is important. To be successful as a hospital CMO, you must have a firm grasp of the bylaws, credentialing and privileging policies, peer review policies, and accreditation processes.

Probably the best experience in these areas comes by serving as a president of the medical staff or the elected chief of staff for the medical staff. These roles often work hand in hand with the CMO and are a great recruiting space for the hospital executive who wants to find an experienced leader who has proven themselves with their peers.

But being a chief of staff is not the only way to get this experience. Long-standing members of the medical executive committee, chairman of the peer review committee, even a department chair gather this experience. Honestly, just studying the bylaws and policies can get you part of the necessary background and it is this practical application of those policies and procedures and putting them to use that makes them stick with you as a leader.

Change Management

The last area of experience that I believe is essential as an incoming CMO is experience in process improvement and change management. Having run a quality committee or a patient safety committee that was tasked with changing an existing process to achieve improved or higher performance is an invaluable experience. Learning how to understand data and metrics, setting up a performance improvement plan that has timelines, assigned accountabilities, and expected outcomes is an incredibly helpful experience to have when you are responsible for the quality and safety of an organization.

There are plenty of other areas where some experience would be useful, including informatics, pharmacy and therapeutics, and utilization management.

A few gaps in experience can be expected in almost all applicants, and those gaps can typically be filled on the job. However, managing the performance of a clinician, having a strong background in medical staff affairs, and having experience with performance improvement are of enough importance that they should be included in the minimum qualifications of the aspiring chief medical officer.

Formal Training and Education

Mark Olszyk provides a comprehensive discussion in Chapter 4 about the benefits and necessity of obtaining an MBA, MHA, or other formal leadership training. There are firmly held opinions on this question of formal training and education. For the purposes of this chapter just be aware that this is an important question for each individual that needs to be answered as part of the discernment process for whether the timing is right for you to take your first CMO job.

Mentor/Coach

One of the best predictors of success for the aspiring CMO is whether they have a mentor and coach. As with the topic of formal education and training, this is such a critical issue that we have devoted an entire chapter to it: Chapter 15 by Gabriella Sherman.

Peer Group

The role of CMO can be a lonely one if not entered into with forethought and planning. As a CMO, you are not quite an administrator, and yet you are no longer viewed as a clinician or clinical leader. The CMO is somewhere in between, and as such, can be left feeling like they have no "tribe" or cohort to belong to. As a CMO, it is important to have a peer group of "like-minded" CMOs. Sharing ideas and initiatives, venting frustrations in a confidential setting, and having a sense of connection professionally are all benefits of a peer group.

Many CMO positions have this sort of peer group built into their organization. As more and more hospitals and medical groups coalesce and consolidate into regional and national organizations, there are likely other CMOs with similar responsibilities, but a different geography area of accountability, who will be those peers.

Most organizations see the value in creating a forum where these leaders with similar accountabilities can connect periodically in person or virtually. It's a chance to share ideas and strategies — both effective and ineffective. This type of internal peer group to commiserate with, to brainstorm with, to have a sense of community with is ideal because you will all likely share the same strategic priorities and objectives and have some shared vocabulary that is unique to your organization.

For stand-alone hospitals and medical groups, there may not be a built-in peer group. If that is the case, you may need to look for camaraderie through professional societies, leadership forums, or professional development courses.

Most CMOs I have worked with eventually build both a formal and informal group of peers over time — a formal group of peers related to the organization itself and an informal group of peers whom they've worked with in the past and may now be with another hospital or health system. Either can be effective; having access to both is ideal. The key point here is that one of the tests of readiness for the CMO job is whether you have access to a peer group to make the job more manageable and more enjoyable.

IS THE ORGANIZATION READY FOR A CMO?

This one is a bit tricky because there is a chicken and egg phenomenon here. You may not be ready for your first CMO job if the organization isn't ready for a CMO. Taking a CMO job that is brand new or without clear accountabilities, without clear measures of success, or without a well-functioning executive team is setting yourself up for failure.

Before you accept your first CMO job, ask questions such as: Is the organization ready to have a CMO? Is this the first time the hospital has had a CMO? What happened to the last CMO? Is there a clear reporting structure and a clear set of job responsibilities? Will you have the necessary resources to accomplish those responsibilities? Who will be your direct reports? Will you have a budget? Will you have an administrative assistant? Is this a turn-around job with poor performance in quality, accreditation, and in financial arenas?

I won't say it is impossible to step into a mess and turn it around, but it's probably not the best environment for your first CMO position. So, part of your readiness is understanding whether there is a CMO job that is adequately resourced, scoped, and supported for you to be successful. You aren't ready for your first CMO job if the organization isn't ready for you.

ARE YOU READY TO LEAVE CLINICAL MEDICINE?

This is probably the toughest question aspiring CMOs encounter and really is the crux of this chapter. We've spent years going to college, medical school, residency, and in many cases a fellowship. Our clinical career is literally decades in the making, and being a physician becomes part of who we are. It is part of our identity to care for patients. Taking a history, developing a diagnosis, creating a care plan, or performing a surgical intervention that will affect the life of another human being is a very tangible and immediate professional reward.

The professional satisfaction of being a physician is not only immediate, but is directed at us individually rather than as a team, department, or hospital. The gratitude and appreciation we feel from a patient or family is a wonderful and amazing part of medicine. It is the professional reward that drives most physicians — more than stature, reputation, and compensation combined. Careers in clinical leadership such as CMO roles see rewards and recognition that span years before they are actualized, and they may never be directed at us individually.

So, when is it time to leave behind your clinical career and pursue a leadership role in medicine? The answer is different for each of us who has seen their career pivot toward the administrative side of healthcare. My advice is to have some intentionality to this decision. Many CMOs, including me, have found ourselves accepting a leadership role that reduced our time devoted to clinical medicine before spending adequate, dedicated time on the discernment.

It is easy to slide into administrative roles without individual perceptiveness. A trusted chief executive asks you to fill a leadership gap and the organizational need is so compelling that you don't always take the time to consider if it is the right time to step away from a part or all of your clinical responsibilities. Is the time right for you to back away from clinical practice?

For some prospective CMOs, the opportunity to affect the system and see the model of care improve so that it influences the lives of many patients, sometimes generations of patients, is the key and we can forgo the immediate rewards of patient care to instead realize the much longer horizon of process improvement.

For others it is the chance to leave a legacy of improvement or stability in a health system that is rife with dysfunction and inefficiencies that outweighs time spent in clinical practice. The chance to improve work conditions and resources for your peers can be a potent motivation. There is tremendous satisfaction in working as part of a team, especially a team that you have selected, nurtured, and inspired. It is the difference between conducting an orchestra and being a terrific soloist. It is not for everyone but if seeing that success in your team is something that gives you a sense of accomplishment, it is probably a significant indication you will find ongoing joy in a CMO position.

There are two reasons one should not leave clinical medicine to pursue the administrative functions of a CMO position. The first is to escape the demands of patient care. If you never loved patient care, if healing and compassion were never aspects of your career and part of your professional persona, then you may not be well suited to influence and lead physicians. We need chief medical officers who love the practice of medicine and want to see it improve.

The second reason not to leave clinical practice is because you think you will now be in charge and can tell others how to practice medicine. The CMO role is one of influence, but certainly not one of absolute authority. As a CMO you can set an agenda and inspire others to excellence and professionalism, but you seldom have the command-and-control latitude to create a future all of your own choosing.

There are many descriptions of what a CMO does on a daily basis. Sometimes it's a salesman, other times a research assistant, a translator, often a cheerleader, and at times a kindergarten teacher (let's all play fair in the sandbox). But it seldom feels like you have full autonomy and authority. It's a job of influence, guidance, and being a role model.

So, at the end of the day, can you set aside the rewards of clinical medicine and channel those energies into system improvement that has a longer timeline and less personal nature in its rewards? Some CMOs try to maintain a residual clinical practice a half day a week or participate in weekend or evening call rotations, but it is difficult to accommodate both.

Staying sharp clinically requires practice, especially in the procedural specialties. Over time your clinical acumen or manual dexterity will slip, so it is usually a bridge into administrative medicine. It's time to judge whether this is the right career path or not. Keeping a remnant of clinical practice for a few years is fully reasonable until you are confident that leadership is the best use of your time and talent.

But don't hold on to the clinical practice too long. As a CMO you are promoting peer review and professionalism. If you've lost your clinical skills and continue to practice, you are not "walking the talk."

I remember well this transition for me. As a hospitalist, it was easy to keep one foot in the clinical arena while I was taking on progressively more administrative responsibilities. A hospitalist job in many urban centers primarily focuses on the cognitive and diagnostic side of medicine. Even common inpatient procedures — central line placement, paracentesis or thoracentesis, joint aspirations, etc. — can be performed by interventional radiologists, intensivists, or anesthesia providers so a hospitalist's job can focus on the diagnostic work-up, management, and discharge coordination.

Thus, losing procedural volume was not as important as it might be for a surgeon. It was easy for me to just swap one of my seven-day clinical stretches and devote it to non-clinical administrative activities. From there it was not difficult to move to providing just occasional weekend or night coverage to accommodate more time for leadership responsibilities.

Finally, moving to just helping on busy days with an admission or a discharge allowed me to keep enough clinical activity to remain privileged, even though it was clear my primary job was now administrative rather than clinical.

I recall one afternoon when my administrative tasks were mostly completed, I paged the triage hospitalist and asked if there was an admission or two that I could help the team with. When the answer was a pause, a ruffling of papers, and then a tentative answer that he thought I could manage a

92-year-old dementia patient who had a UTI and probably needed nursing home placement, it became clear to me that perhaps my time was better spent improving the system of care rather than on the modest help I could provide caring for one ailing patient.

During the next credentialing cycle, I dropped my admitting privileges. It had been an eight-year journey of gradually reducing my clinical time, and I was ready to devote myself fully to administrative leadership.

Do I miss the clinical work? Almost every day. And that is probably why I make a halfway decent administrative leader for my organization. I participate in regular multidisciplinary rounds with my clinicians, stay current with my license and board certification, and do a fair amount of shadowing clinicians while they do their work. It is not a substitute for clinical practice, but it partially scratches that itch and my need to stay relevant clinically.

Be prepared for this decision and the transition away from clinical practice to be a journey for you as well. There will be days when you wonder if you made the right choice and flip through listings of clinical positions in your area that are open; there also will be days when you see consensus develop on improved workflows, a physician career saved by succeeding in a performance improvement plan, or when your hospital becomes CMS 5-star rated that you will be reassured it has all been worth it. It takes time to see the trade-off value, but being a CMO is an incredibly rewarding career.

IS YOUR FAMILY READY FOR THE TRANSITION?

Let's not forget the most important people in this discernment over the timing of becoming a CMO. Your spouse, your children, and perhaps aging parents need to be front and center in this consideration. You may find the time demands of a CMO position are less than your clinical practice, but I can assure you that at times they will feel like more.

In moving to a CMO job, you may finally forgo the every-fourth-night calls and monthly weekend hospital calls that defined your clinical career for more of a Monday to Friday job. But be aware that those Monday to Friday weekdays that often start with the anesthesia department meeting at 6:30 a.m. and may not conclude until after an evening Medical Executive Committee meeting finishes at 9:00 p.m.

There tend to be more dinner meetings and more out-of-town travel for system, state, or national organizations that your hospital wants you to attend. And even though you are not "on call" and expected to respond to patient care in the hospital on a regular basis, there are plenty of times when disruptive physician behavior, clinical errors, or unannounced visits by regulatory agencies send you to the hospital unplanned.

You can be a great parent and a great CMO. You can coach T-ball or soccer and be a CMO. You can be an incredible son or daughter and provide care supervision to aging parents. But having a spouse, friend, or sibling who understands your role and is willing to cover some of the home front when you are pressed into hospital or medical group responsibilities is helpful and something to think through and plan for ahead of time.

The other side of the equation is setting boundaries with your clinical leadership team and ensuring there is effective coverage when you take time off. Share your calendars, be aware of each other's home obligations, and create an environment of mutual support in the C-suite. It will serve you and your team well.

The guidance here is that you understand your time commitments in your CMO position and have an honest discussion with those important to you on the home front. The support you have from these individuals will be the difference between feeling torn by competing obligations and being able to focus and succeed in your leadership role.

ARE YOU READY TO LEAD?

If whether to leave clinical practice is the toughest question, this is the most important question: Are you ready to lead? Healthcare today does not need reluctant or passive leaders who lack a vision and passion for the profession. We have too many serious problems to see CMO jobs held by folks who are placeholders finishing the last few years of their career in an administrative role.

We need chief medical officers who have a "fire in their belly" to transform healthcare and the patience to plan, build support, and work a change process that can take years. We need CMOs dedicated to developing the next generation of physician leaders. We need CMOs who are ardent supporters of professionalism. We need CMOs who play an active role in clinician wellness and mitigate the epidemic of burnout in our ranks. We need CMOs who are passionate advocates of our patients and are relentless in their pursuit of quality and safety for those under our care.

If you have a nagging sense that just providing great care at the bedside will be insufficient to the patients you care for, if you find yourself bothered by inefficiencies and ineffective clinical strategies, if you see substandard care and it leaves you stirred to action … it may be that leadership is calling your name.

Stepping into a CMO role can be hugely rewarding, but you have to want it. You have to want to make care better by leading your colleagues and transforming the care model. That is the essence of the successful CMO: You must want to lead.

IS THE TIMING EVER RIGHT?

We have covered quite a bit of ground and I have given you much to consider before you judge yourself ready for your first CMO job. You might be thinking the time will never be right to transition to a CMO job if you are waiting to have all these topics and concerns answered in the affirmative. And many successful CMOs, including me, will tell you that we weren't fully ready when we stepped into our first CMO job, and yet we did just fine.

The reality is that having each criterion fully secured and each box checked may be overly cautious and prevent you from taking the plunge into the world of physician leadership. So please consider this chapter with a balance of both wanting to not make a rushed or poorly considered decision, and the knowledge that if you have answered most of these questions in the affirmative and have strong sense of purpose and dedication to the role, you will in all likelihood be successful as a CMO.

But also recognize that for some of you, waiting is the better course of action. It is common to worry that if you pass on the position, the opportunity may never again present itself. But the reality is, CMO positions come open relatively often. The average tenure in a hospital CMO job is measured in years, not decades. Physician leaders choose to move to system roles, back to clinical practice, to another hospital or health system. Unfortunately, sometimes these roles get reorganized and eliminated only to reappear two years down the road.

The constant is that it is hard to effectively run a hospital, medical group, or health plan without effective senior physician leadership that most often comes in the form of a well-prepared CMO. So, patience is sometimes in your best interest. Get yourself prepared. Wait for the right role. Then jump in and have a wonderful career as a chief medical officer.

PART II

Feedback from Chief Executives and Others Hiring

CHAPTER 3

The Importance of Experience

Rex Hoffman, MD, MBA, FACHE, CPE

WHEN I WAS A MEDICAL director exploring about what I needed to do to be considered a serious applicant for a chief medical officer job, a chief executive encouraged me to get experience on the Utilization Management (UM) Committee, Quality Management Committee, and Credentials Committee. As a radiation oncologist at the time, I had limited exposure to these committees, but once I made my mind up that I wanted to be a CMO, I got involved with all of them. As a chief medical officer a year or so later, I was glad I did.

This was my path; however, the chief executives or senior chief medical officers who hire CMOs may define experience differently. Consequently, the contributors to this book created a 10-question survey that was sent to 10 chief executives, three health system chief medical officers, and two regional chief medical officers. Possible responses were Strongly Disagree, Disagree, Neutral, Agree, and Strongly Agree.

WHAT EXPERIENCE IS IMPORTANT?

Here is what we learned about what chief executives look for when hiring a CMO:

1. How important is it to have previously been a chief of staff?

A common perception is that you need to be a chief of staff before you will be taken seriously for a CMO job. This is false! Our survey responses to this question were split with 50% "neutral" or "disagree" and 50% "agree." So, it is really 50-50!

This result is not surprising, since not every chief of staff has the skillset to be an effective chief medical officer. Chiefs of staff are often well-versed in what is important to the medical staff, but not as much about what is important to administration. There are exceptions though, with some working very closely with their administrative counterparts to accomplish the medical staff's priorities without it being detrimental to the administration.

The ability to work across the aisle to benefit both sides is an attractive characteristic some chiefs of staff exemplify. Effective chief medical officers need to be able to walk such a narrow line by acting as a liaison between the medical staff and administration. At the end of the day, though, they are administration, so this is where their primary focus needs to be.

It is also important to consider that the respondents' answers to this question were likely biased by the chiefs of staff the respondents have worked with. Not all of them display the traits and characteristics that are vital to a CMO and thus although they may be effective chiefs of staff, this does not necessarily correlate with them being effective CMOs. I have worked with some chiefs of staff who would make great CMOs and others who would not.

Of the 11 chief medical officers I work most closely with today, only two have been chiefs of staff.

2. How important is it to have served on the Medical Executive Committee?

Our respondents indicated that membership on the Medical Executive Committee (MEC) is a bonus: 40% agree and another 40% strongly agree. Serving on this committee exposes you to the most important decision that leaders on the medical staff and in administration face and provides exposure to the elements of decision-making, including the importance of compromising when necessary.

Having this experience will better prepare you to deal with decisions you will likely have to make as a chief medical officer. Being on the MEC also highlights the importance of relationships among the various medical staff departments and strategies for navigating the politics that may arise on this important decision-making committee.

Being a leader on the MEC also puts you on a different level with your physician peers. As a leader, you will be viewed as an advocate for your colleagues and must lead by example. Whether you like it or not, other physicians will be watching your every move and look to you to stand up for them on certain issues. Being successful on both fronts will prepare you well as a chief medical officer. After all, as a CMO, you, too, will have your every move and action critiqued and will be expected to speak up during important discussions.

Being a member of the Medical Executive Committee implies that you are the chief of staff, vice chief of staff, a department chair, a chair of a major committee, or have been elected as an at-large member. If you are a department chair, that in itself is an impressive feat and requires you to work closely with the chief medical officer when it comes to addressing inappropriate physician behavior within your department.

In addition, being a department chair or a chair of a major committee means that you will be required to moderate important meetings on campus, which is another skill you will want to fine tune if you aspire to be a chief medical officer, since CMOs often facilitate meetings in the organization.

3. How important is it to have been on the Utilization Management Committee?

Utilization management is a major area of focus for CMOs. When I queried the chief executive on what I could do to make myself an attractive candidate for a future CMO job, he suggested I get involved with the Utilization Management (UM) Committee, Quality Management Committee, and Credentials Committee, adding, "If you only have time for one, participate on the UM committee. Doing so will distinguish you from physicians who are not familiar with this work or have not taken the time to learn it."

I followed his advice, and not only did it likely give me a leg up on the competition when I applied for a CMO job, but it also prepared me for the work when I became a CMO. By familiarizing yourself with the UM Committee you learn about length of stay, avoidable days, care delays, readmissions, condition code 44 data, regulatory and compliance updates, Medicare 1-day stays, appeals, denials, drugs and biologicals, CMS PEPPER, observation data, and other process improvement opportunities as deemed appropriate.

At the heart of this work is the focus on overutilization, underutilization, and misutilization of resources. As CMO, decreasing the length of stay is my top priority; understanding the importance of clinical documentation (and CDI queries) and how to interact effectively with case management is also very important.

Our respondents concur: 70% said they agree and 20% said they strongly agree about the importance of serving on the UM Committee. Based on these results, I strongly recommend you participate on your UM committee if you want to be a chief medical officer.

Some physicians who are considering becoming chief medical officers also take on the role of physician advisor — essentially a subject matter expert in the areas of utilization management and clinical documentation. In these capacities, they work closely with the case management department and the chief medical officer. Talk about an opportunity to get yourself noticed! I have my physician advisor on speed dial and speak with her several times a week.

4. How important is it to have been on a Quality Management Committee?

According to our respondents, it is very important: 30% agreed and a whopping 60% strongly agreed. This makes sense, since overseeing the quality of care in the organization is one of the most important responsibilities of a CMO. Being on this committee will introduce you to the key measures CMOs are responsible for: hospital-acquired infections, hand hygiene, and CMS quality metrics, to name a few.

Membership on this committee also will introduce you to other key players in the organization who focus on this work, including the infection prevention team, quality team, and physician and nursing leaders who have taken a leadership role in this area.

What would be even more impressive is if you became the physician champion for one of the quality metrics the hospital is prioritizing. This would allow you to become a subject matter expert and thus be seen as a key leader in an area that is important to your CMO and those they work closely with.

Therefore, I strongly recommend that as a practicing physician you serve on this committee when in clinical practice. After all, it will not only serve you and your patients well to know what is going on from a quality perspective but will make you a more desirable candidate for that CMO job you are seeking.

Personally, this year has been a boon for us at Providence Holy Cross, with several accolades coming our way, including CMS 5-star, Healthgrades

50 Best Hospitals when it comes to clinical excellence in several different specialties, and being recognized by Becker's as a top hospital for quality of care. And believe me, my CEO and I both know which physician leaders have been instrumental in helping us achieve these awards. Talk about getting a leg up or a good letter of recommendation when they apply for a future CMO job.

5. How important is it to have been on the Credentials Committee?

Respondents to our survey indicated that serving on this committee was important as well, with 50% saying they agree and an additional 30% said they strongly agree. Getting credentials and subsequent privileges to join a medical staff is serious business and must be treated as such. Being able to scrutinize medical staff applications to ensure that a physician is well suited to join the medical staff is an important skillset to maintain the integrity of the medical staff. After all, the medical staff is only as strong as its weakest physician.

Serving on the Credentials Committee exposes one to all types of issues that may accompany an application, such as an applicant with multiple open claims against them, reports of driving while under the influence, or a felony conviction, to name a few.

Sometimes a difficult decision needs to be made that will prevent an applicant from joining the medical staff for reasons that are in the best interest of the medical staff's reputation. Alternatively, sometimes a difficult decision will need to be made where a physician with some strikes against them will be allowed to join the medical staff. After all, if a medical staff develops a reputation for being difficult to join, such a reputation would inevitably prevent the medical staff from attracting good candidates and thus create voids when it comes to certain specialties. In the long run, this will only harm the community being cared for by the physicians.

Another aspect of being on the Credentials Committee that sets one up well to be a chief medical officer is the relationship with the medical staff office that oversees the Credentials Committee. It is a major plus to have the medical staff officers speak favorably about you with regard to being conscientious, fair, non-biased, honest, and moral. And medical staff officers talk, so if you plan to apply for a chief medical officer job at a hospital other than your own, know that the hospital at which you are applying will reach out to the medical staff office you are coming from to learn about your reputation.

6. How important is it to have been a medical director?

Our respondents were lukewarm on this one; 40% said they were neutral and 60% agreed it was important. Being a medical director often implies you are a subject matter expert in your respective area. One's expertise in a field does not necessarily correlate with any of the functions of being an effective chief medical officer, so this response is not surprising.

Having been a medical director of radiation oncology for 11 years and now a CMO, I tend to agree that my role as a medical director did not in any way prepare me for being a good CMO. The only overlap between the two positions is that as a medical director, I was familiar with the content of my medical directorship and my medical group's professional service agreement, since I signed off on both documents.

Since chief medical officers play a major role in creating the language in medical directorships when it comes to setting goals and evaluating medical directors performance annually, it did help to know what is contained in these agreements and how they are managed.

As a medical director, the best way to impress the chief medical officer or other executive you are working with is to meet (and exceed) all of your goals, which demonstrates to them that you take your job seriously. In the end, chief medical officers can always change their medical directors if they don't believe they are providing value to the organization.

Although our respondents did not consider being a medical director as overly important, I encourage you to aspire to become one for a couple of reasons. First, it shows that you are a subject matter expert in an area which administration will inevitably lean on at some point.

Second, it guarantees that you will interact with your chief medical officer when you set your goals for the year and when they evaluate your performance annually. During these meetings, be prepared and show the chief medical officer that your role provides value to the organization. They will appreciate you and know that you are aligned with their priorities when it comes to your area of expertise.

One aspect of managing medical directorships that is important for a chief medical officer but is not necessarily learned as a medical director is the art of negotiation. After all, chief medical officers need to be able to effectively negotiate the rate and maximum number of hours a medical director is slated for in the agreement. This is a skill that must be learned. As a medical director, you get a chance firsthand to see how your chief medical officer handles this situation.

7. How important is it to have been on the medical staff at the hospital where you want to be the chief medical officer?

It's not considered to be as important as you might expect— about 50-50. In the past, popular or well-respected physicians on a medical staff had a leg up when it came to being considered for a chief medical officer position. After all, they had already established relationships with the key physician leaders in the organization and knew what the priorities were and administration got to see how effective they were in navigating difficult issues and see firsthand if they could represent administration in achieving its goals. However, it is clear from the responses that some chief executives prefer going outside of the organization to bring in a new perspective or new set of eyes and ears to help them with their agendas.

Regardless of these findings, I still encourage you to put your best foot forward in your organization and show that you are a team player and are aligned with the administration's priorities, if possible. You never know what chief executives will prioritize when conducting their search for a CMO, but one thing is for sure: You want them to be aware of who you are and that you have demonstrated that you can be counted on when leading an effort in the organization.

The alternative is possible too, however. Since you are a known entity in your organization and have a certain reputation, you may not be considered a good fit for what they are looking for. If you are viewed as a troublemaker, someone who is difficult to get along with, or have demonstrated that you are not a team player when it comes to discussing issues with administration, it will be far more difficult for you to be considered seriously for the chief medical officer job when it becomes available.

Personally, I have seen this work both ways. Of the 11 chief medical officers I work with most closely, four came from their respective medical staffs.

8. How important is it to have previously been a chief medical officer?

It's not very important, according to our respondents: 50% were either neural, disagreed, or strongly disagreed. All CMOs need to start somewhere, and I get the sense from several of our correspondents that they prefer to work with a new, untainted CMO whom they can mold to their way of thinking and manage right out of the gate. Having previously been a CMO does not necessarily mean you were a good one and therefore it is not surprising our survey takers answered the way they did.

Alternatively, 50% did agree or strongly agree with the importance of previously being a CMO, so if you were previously an effective chief medical officer and did a great job, this will help you when searching for your next chief medical officer job. Inevitably, those chief executives who consider hiring a physician who was previously a chief medical officer will check with the CMO's prior supervisor to see how effective they had been in this role. So, if you were previously a CMO and now are looking to move to a new CMO job, make sure you are leaving on good terms.

Other areas you will have wanted to excel at include decreasing length of stay, effectively addressing inappropriate physician behavior, and demonstrating respect and integrity.

Sometimes, despite exhibiting exemplary behavior, a chief medical officer does not hit it off with their chief executive and they need to part ways. If this applies to you, leave on good terms. Any future employer will not only reach out to your prior employer but ask you why you left. Be prepared to address this truthfully in your interview.

OTHER CONSIDERATIONS

Survey questions 9 and 10 were around whether being a Certified Physician Executive (CPE) provided value and whether there was a benefit to obtaining a Master of Business Administration or Master of Health Administration. Mark Olszyk addresses these two questions in Chapter 4.

Another area that was not part of our survey but that I recommend you pursue is getting to know your chief medical officer. Learn what their priorities are, how they spend their time, and what keeps them awake at night. Although not all chief medical officers have the same priorities, spend their time the same way, or fret over the same things, it will give you a better sense as to what life is like as a CMO.

It is also important to be the doctor they think of when they think about a successor or a physician leader they could see themselves wanting to help when the next chief medical officer job becomes open.

IN SUMMATION

In summation, based on their responses to this survey, it appears that those who hire chief medical officers felt strongly that a physician aspiring to become a CMO should spend time participating on the Utilization Management Committee, Quality Management Committee, and Credentials Committee. Each of these committees exposes physicians to important aspects of what they would be dealing with as a CMO.

Being on the Medical Executive Committee is a nice bonus. Because it is not always easy to get on the MEC, getting elected to this prestigious committee in your hospital reflects how respected you are among your peers, which is important. On the other side of the coin, membership on the MEC often is extremely political, so the opportunity to serve on this committee may be outside of one's realistic reach. Don't let this discourage you.

Reach out to the chair of the UM Committee, Quality Management Committee, and Credentials Committee and see if you can participate going forward. This will expose you to important issues that you will need to better understand as a chief medical officer and will show those you encounter in the application process that you are aware of what a CMO does.

If for some reason you are not able to join one of these committees or the committee does not exist in your organization, I strongly recommend you ask your chief medical officer which committees they feel are most important and where they would suggest you spend your time, since you are interested in potentially becoming a CMO some day. At a minimum, they will be impressed and will likely want to help you. That can't hurt.

CHAPTER 4

The Importance of Additional Degrees and Certifications

Mark D. Olszyk, MD, MBA, CPE, FACEP, FACHE, FAAPL, FFSMB

E XPLORING THE MERIT OF PURSUING an additional degree begins with defining the degree's "value." This inquiry can encompass various aspects, including the financial return on investment. It involves assessing how much additional revenue could be generated over the remainder of one's career compared to the expense of obtaining the additional degree.

Additionally, one must consider the opportunity costs associated with forgoing other potential actions or pursuits. Pursuing an MBA, for instance, requires a substantial time commitment over a couple of years, which could alternatively be used for moonlighting or other activities that offer immediate financial benefits or personal satisfaction.

Determining the value of an additional degree is complex and does not easily lend itself to a simple cost/benefit analysis. Program costs vary widely between degrees and certifications, as well as among programs offering the same degree or credential. Some programs are more efficient and can be completed in a shorter time frame of one or two years. Therefore, while I will present some fundamental considerations, ultimately, individuals should conduct their own detailed calculations.

Still, value extends beyond financial aspects. There is intrinsic value in the pleasure of learning and mastering a subject, which may be a personal goal. After evaluating the costs, time commitment, and potential benefits, individuals may conclude that pursuing an additional degree is not worthwhile.

Many individuals are likely interested in the value proposition of degrees such as an MBA, CPE, or other master's degrees. To provide a comprehensive view, we will also consider other degrees that complement a medical degree. Table 1 outlines an approximation of the cost, timeline, common applications, and, if available, the number of physicians who hold each degree or credential.

TABLE 1. Overview of Common Degrees and Credentials

Degree	Cost	Time	Usage	Number of Physicians Who Have the Credential (if known)
MBA	$26,000–$100,000	2-3 years	Leadership in a healthcare organization	
MHA	$36,000–$63,000	2-3 years	Medical leadership in a healthcare organization	
MPH	$20,000–$83,000	2-3 years	Public health position	
MMM	$15,000–$70,000	12-18 months	Leadership in a health plan, ACO, or CIN	
CPE	$16,500 Much less if you already have an MBA	12-15 months	Physician leadership in a healthcare organization	4,000
FACHE	Cost varies $225 for the exam after meeting the requirements	5 years of management experience	Leadership in a healthcare organization	2,319, including 644 chief medical officers
PhD	$50,000–$294,000	3-8 years	Research, academia	2,000
JD	$220,000	2-3 years	Law, academia	6,000

Information about degrees is readily available online. See References 1–7.

RETURN ON INVESTMENT

In examining the financial aspects of pursuing additional degrees in the medical field, we initially consider the return on investment, starting with the cost of medical school. The tuition for medical school varies, and the subsequent lifelong remuneration hinges on factors such as one's specialty, location, and length of career. For instance, an academic primary care physician in one region may earn considerably less than an orthopedic surgeon or a cosmetic surgeon in another area, with the earnings difference potentially reaching five-fold.

While many of us did not pursue medical school solely for the financial prospects, viewing it instead as a vocation or calling, it can still be viewed as a valuable investment.

To illustrate, let's consider a primary care physician who earns $4.8 million gross over 30 years (at an annual rate of $160,000) with total medical school debt calculated at the current nationwide average of $369,229.[8] This scenario yields a return on investment of 43.3% annually. Even a calculation of the net return on investment presents a favorable outcome.

Conversely, an orthopedic surgeon starting their career with an annual salary of $400,000 would accumulate $12 million in earnings over 30 years, representing an even more favorable return on investment.

For physicians considering pursuing additional degrees, particularly those who wish to incorporate administrative, regulatory, or research aspects into their careers, various options are available. Common degrees include master of public health, master of healthcare administration, master of business administration, and the MD/PhD. Physicians may also choose to pursue a degree in law.

These additional degrees can be obtained through combined programs while still in medical school or later in one's career. Pursuing such degrees full-time while in medical school may prove to be a more cost-effective and expedient path. Many medical schools offer MD/PhD, MD/MPH, or MD/JD options.

For physicians interested in medical leadership, the Certified Physician Executive (CPE) credential granted by the American Association for Physician Leadership and fellowship in the American College of Healthcare Executives (FACHE) are noteworthy considerations. These credentials can often be satisfied by holding a master's degree.

When evaluating whether to pursue additional degrees or credentials, it is essential to consider each program's prerequisites, applications, requirements, and conferred benefits. Additionally, one should assess how each degree or credential is perceived by peers or hiring authorities, as this may impact one's competitive edge in the job market.

Master of Business Administration (MBA)

A sizable proportion of newly graduated medical doctors often lack fundamental knowledge in staff management, financial modeling, organizational leadership, and the profitability dynamics of hospitals or clinical practices. Acquiring an MBA equips doctors with practical tools to address many pressing issues in healthcare today and provides a robust foundation for leadership development.

Requirements:
- Bachelor's degree from a recognized institution.
- GPA of at least 3.0.
- Three years or more of experience in the healthcare or human services industries.
- GRE or GMAT scores or waiver based on experience.
- Personal statement.
- Letters of reference.

Having both medical and business degrees can offer an advantage, particularly in hospital administration, where top executives typically have MBAs. A study found that hospitals led by doctors as CEOs performed 25% better in quality scores compared to those led by non-medical executives.[9] This underscores the importance of integrating clinical and managerial knowledge in healthcare institutions.

Dr. Toby Cosgrove, CEO of Cleveland Clinic, emphasized the significance of credibility and peer-to-peer credibility, suggesting that physicians leading hospitals have a firsthand understanding of the needs of their colleagues, which enhances their credibility and insights.[10]

An MBA can benefit physician leaders by providing:
- Understanding of how economic supply and demand dynamics impact the healthcare sector.
- Enhanced comprehension of accreditation, regulatory licensure, and compliance standards specific to healthcare.
- Exposure to various perspectives on healthcare management decisions.
- Familiarity with industry-specific technologies.
- Ability to identify, understand, and devise solutions for key sector challenges.
- Networking opportunities with other medical specialists.

Within the next decade, the Bureau of Labor Statistics predicts a 28% growth in occupational outlooks for medical health services managers as technical aspects of medicine increase and populations age. About 54,700 openings for medical and health services managers are projected each year, on average, over the decade.[11]

One of the best-paying jobs in the medical field is that of hospital administrator. A 2014 *New York Times* study found that hospital administration and CEO salaries were far higher than those of general practitioners. The mean yearly income of a hospital administrator was $237,000, which was about $50,000 higher than that of the typical clinical physician, who typically made $185,000.[12] A 2018 study by *Clinical Orthopaedics and Related Research* found that nonprofit hospital CEO salaries grew by 93% from 2005 to 2015.[13,14]

The trend of universities offering combined MD/MBA programs is on the rise, increasing from six programs to 65 over the last two decades. These programs allow students to complete both degrees in four to five years, offering a more streamlined and cost-effective path compared to pursuing the degrees separately.

While an MBA can be valuable, it may not be necessary for everyone. Those aiming to own a private practice may find that a few business classes provide sufficient skills. However, for those interested in hospital administration, the additional cost of obtaining an MHA or MBA is justified by the potential increase in salary and career opportunities.

Doug Bennett, writing in AMN Healthcare, says, "As medicine becomes more of a business, it is essential for physicians to develop a good framework for understanding the ever-changing drivers that can affect them, including insurance reimbursement, budgeting and financial modeling, IT security, marketing strategies, and healthcare law, to name just a few. MBA programs can also help physicians learn how to communicate more persuasively and effectively with other decision-makers, including board members and potential investors."[15]

Average Cost: $26,000–$100,000[16]

Master of Healthcare Administration (MHA)

Similar to MBA programs. MHA programs typically require two years to complete. However, the cost of obtaining an MHA is generally lower than that of an MBA. While MBA graduates, on average, earn more than their MHA counterparts, an MHA degree provides graduates with a broad array of job opportunities in public health, policy, and public service within the healthcare sector.[17]

The MHA curriculum, like that of an MBA, includes business courses covering management, finance, strategy, law, and ethics. However, the focus of an MHA is on roles in operations and clinical management. An MBA may offer more extensive training in finance and analytics, making it more valuable for individuals interested in careers in marketing, finance, or investing. It is worth noting MHA programs typically do not provide the same networking opportunities that we see in MBA programs.[18]

Requirements:
- Bachelor's degree from a recognized institution.
- GPA of at least 3.0.
- Three years or more of experience in the healthcare or human services industries.
- GRE or GMAT scores.
- Personal statement.
- Letters of reference.

Average Cost: $36,720

Growth of physicians vs healthcare administrators

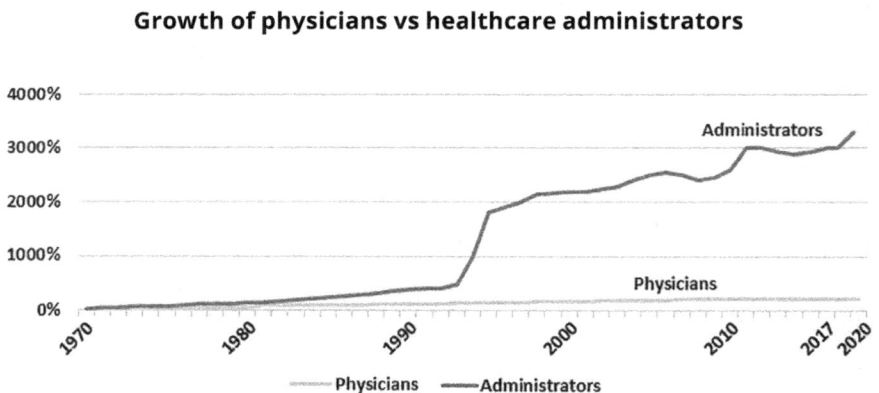

FIGURE 1. The number of physicians in the United States grew 150% between 1975 and 2010, roughly in keeping with population growth, while the number of healthcare administrators increased 3,200% for the same time period. The trend continued over the next decade, albeit not as steeply.[19,20]

Master of Public Health (MPH)

The MD/MPH dual degree program is an ideal choice for students interested in understanding how social determinants of health influence access to and quality of care. This program typically spans five years and allows students to complete core MPH courses covering subjects such as epidemiology, biostatistics, and health policy and management.

Requirements:
- Bachelor's degree from a recognized institution.
- 3.0 GPA on a 4.0 scale or 83-86% at the undergraduate level (science-related degree).
- Minimum one-year course in calculus, algebra, general or human biology (depends upon specialization and university).
- GRE test score (varies with the university).
- Personal statement.
- Letters of reference.
- Work experience of 2–5 years for best MS colleges in the United States.[2]

Graduates of the MD/MPH program are well-equipped to work in various public health settings, including local health departments, state health departments, and national organizations like the Centers for Disease Control and Prevention or the United States Public Health Service Commissioned Corps. They can contribute to addressing national health priorities and implementing effective public health interventions.

Career opportunities for MD/MPH graduates include roles such as community outreach coordinators, health educators, health engagement marketing managers, public policy coordinators, substance abuse counselors, clinical dietitians, healthcare administrators, epidemiologists, health educators, and environmental health scientists. These professionals play critical roles in promoting health equity, disease prevention, and improving overall population health.[21]

Average Cost: $20,000–$82,000

Master of Medical Management (MMM)

The master of medical management (MMM) degree gained popularity in the early 1990s, coinciding with the implementation of managed care by health plans and large medical groups. These programs are typically shorter than traditional MBAs, often completed in 12 to 18 months. Some programs have since transitioned to the title of "healthcare MBA."[22]

MMM programs are designed for physicians with considerable healthcare leadership experience seeking additional education in business and finance. These programs prepare physician leaders to manage programs that bridge the gap between healthcare providers and insurers.

Requirements:
- Bachelor's degree from a recognized institution.
- 3-5 years of experience in healthcare.
- GRE or GMAT scores (varies with the university).

The unique benefits of MMM programs are particularly valuable for physician leaders aspiring to become chief medical officers (CMOs) of health plans, accountable care organizations (ACOs), or clinically integrated networks (CINs) that assume financial risk. The curriculum focuses on managing the total cost of care, understanding the revenue cycle of healthcare, interpreting actuarial information, and predicting healthcare expenditures for patient populations.

Average Cost: $25,000–$70,000

Certified Physician Executive (CPE)

The American Association for Physician Leadership (AAPL) is the only organization that grants a credential for medical leadership studies. The CPE designation communicates one's business acumen to colleagues, current and future employers, recruiters, and others. It endorses your ability to lead large groups, manage budgets, address HR challenges, and apply strategic business insights. The CPE curriculum provides you with the knowledge, skills, and core competencies in key areas to transition into a wide array of leadership roles.

Several courses in the curriculum culminate in the Capstone project, which AAPL emphasizes as the most impactful aspect of the program, which takes about 12–15 months to complete. Core classes consist of finance, health law, resolving conflict, high reliability, change management, managing physician performance, negotiation, communication, building teams, influence, and quality.

If you already have an MBA, you only need to take two out of five courses and complete the Capstone to earn the CPE. In addition, you need two years of leadership experience and one year of membership in AAPL. To be eligible for the CPE Capstone, the candidate must:

- Be a licensed MD or DO.
- Be an active AAPL member for at least one year.
- Have at least two years of healthcare leadership experience and significant managerial oversight.
- Be licensed to practice and be (or have been) board-certified in a clinical specialty recognized by the American Board of Medical Specialties, the American Osteopathic Association, or an equivalent commission in the country in which they live.
- Have three years of experience in clinical practice beyond residency and fellowship training.
- Complete the CPE curriculum or hold a qualifying graduate management degree such as an MBA, MMM, MNA, MPH, MS-HQSM, or MS in management. CPE candidates who do not have a master's level management degree must complete a core curriculum of 14 courses totaling 125 CME hours.[23,24]

In this context, leadership is defined as having responsibility for establishing, articulating, and executing the team and/or organizational vision. This includes coordinating and balancing the various interests of all team members and stakeholders and having the ability to lead and participate in strategy, finance, staffing, recruitment, hiring, firing, and other executive duties.

To participate in the CPE program, participants must attest to experience in these areas: talent management, data management, fiscal responsibilities, and organizational impact.

There are approximately 4,100 CPEs worldwide.

To assess the impact of the credential, AAPL tracked the outcomes of program graduates in 2023 by surveying physician leaders who had completed their CPE credential.

The survey revealed that CPE graduates had utilized the skills and knowledge they gained to enhance patient outcomes through quality and safety initiatives, as well as improve organizational outcomes, such as financial performance, cultural change, physician engagement, and leadership during the COVID-19 pandemic.

Survey respondents were able to link their performance to measurable outcomes in various ways, including improved quality and safety metrics; enhanced patient, staff, or physician satisfaction; reduced employee turnover; organizational or program growth; and financial gains or savings.

The survey included 365 respondents who held various positions in different types of organizations. More than half of them worked in local hospitals/health systems or multi-hospital systems, and more than half held the titles of "medical director" or "chief medical officer."

The respondents overwhelmingly agreed that their participation in the CPE program had supported organizational improvements. A vast majority (90.3%) of CPE holders agreed that "The AAPL CPE program empowered me to achieve leadership goals both individually and organizationally."

Moreover, 70% of respondents agreed that "The organizational changes I made were largely a result of the knowledge and skills acquired from the AAPL CPE program."

Average Cost: $16,500

Fellow of the American College of Healthcare Executives (FACHE)

The American College of Healthcare Executives grants a fellowship credential as well, but it is not exclusive to physicians. The credential:
- Provides recognition as a leader among leaders in healthcare management.
- Demonstrates competency in all areas of healthcare management.
- Signifies lifelong commitment to change and improvement.

Requirements:
- Current membership in the ACHE with one year of tenure as an ACHE member, faculty associate, or international associate. Student associate membership does not count toward tenure.
- A master's degree or other post-baccalaureate degree.
- Current employment in an executive healthcare management-level position AND have a minimum of five years of healthcare management experience.
- Two references.

Juris Doctor (JD)

Tracking the exact number of physician-lawyers in the United States is challenging, but estimates from 2002 suggest that between 1,500 and 6,000 individuals hold both MD/JD or DO/JD degrees. The path to becoming a physician-lawyer is gaining traction, particularly as healthcare issues become more entwined with government, managed care, and legal proceedings.

Combined JD/MD programs typically span six years and provide students with a comprehensive education from both schools. Some credits may transfer between the two programs, allowing students to efficiently acquire the knowledge and skills necessary for both professions.

Academia, hospital administration, government, and public policy are among the fields where professionals with JD and MD degrees often work. Some become forensic pathologists, in-house counsel at biotechnology research firms, or go into medical malpractice litigation, food and drug law, medical ethics, or intellectual property law that involves medical devices.[25-27]

Average national salary ranges for careers with medical and law degrees are:[16]

- Medical professor: $105,000–$187,000
- Healthcare or malpractice attorney: $90,000–$240,000
- Intellectual property attorney: $110,000–$200,000
- Private law firm name partner: $320,000–$360,000

MD/PhD

In the United States, approximately 20,000 individuals hold both MD and PhD degrees, with around 600 new MD/PhD degrees conferred each year. This dual degree typically requires an additional three or four years beyond the MD. Many MD/PhD graduates pursue careers in academia and research.

Interestingly, MD/PhD students often select medical specialties with lower-than-average compensation compared to their MD counterparts. For instance, a national study on MD/PhD program outcomes revealed that 14% of MD/PhD alumni choose pathology, a specialty chosen by only 1% of MDs; only 7.4% choose surgery, in contrast to 12% of MDs.

The decision to pursue a PhD in addition to an MD is influenced by various factors, including financial considerations. Some argue that it does not make sense to self-finance the PhD portion of the program, suggesting that external funding sources are preferable.[17]

According to AAMC data, nearly 80% of MD/PhD program graduates have career paths consistent with physician-scientist training, with more than three-quarters of graduates conducting research.[26, 28, 29]

MY JOURNEY

Upon completing my residency in 2000, I anticipated an end to formal education and standardized tests, aside from continuing medical education (CME) and board certification/recertification. Throughout my life, education had been punctuated by quizzes, exams, papers, and filling in bubbles on Scantron sheets. Finally, with an MD after my name, I could focus on practicing medicine and earning a living, with no plans for additional post-nominals except for fellow status in the American College of Emergency Physicians (FACEP).

However, my trajectory changed when, just one year after residency, I assumed leadership of the emergency department at Naval Hospital Great Lakes. Managing an annual budget, overseeing active-duty and civilian physicians, nurses, and hospital corpsmen, and coordinating a busy EMS service required skills in supply chain management, project management, human resources, finance, scheduling, and delegation that were not part of my medical training. Despite the challenges, I found the role exhilarating and realized a talent for medical leadership, spurring a desire for further education.

Fortunately, the G.I. Bill provided an opportunity for me to pursue a master's degree in business administration (MBA). The increasing availability of online courses allowed me to balance work, practice, and family responsibilities. Additionally, leadership training courses offered by various organizations, including the American College of Emergency Physicians, the Navy, and the Department of Veterans Affairs, introduced me to the American College of Healthcare Executives and the American Association for Physician Leadership, of which I became a member.

My MBA largely fulfilled the requirements for fellowship in the American College of Healthcare Executives, with the remaining prerequisites easily met through additional coursework. While the MD degree undoubtedly opened doors for me, the MBA proved to be the most recognized and beneficial in medical executive positions. The Certified Physician Executive (CPE) credential provided invaluable training and networking opportunities, complemented by my fellowship in the American Association for Physician Leadership, which required years of commitment, mentorship, published articles, and active participation in the organization.

CONCLUSION

In conclusion, the decision for physician executives to pursue additional degrees or certifications, such as a master's, PhD, JD, CPE, or FACHE, should be carefully considered based on several factors. These include internal motivations and interests, time constraints, cost, opportunities for advancement, and the evolving demands of the healthcare industry.

Each individual must assess these factors to determine the most beneficial path for their career development and professional fulfillment. By making a well-informed decision, physician executives can enhance their leadership skills, expand their knowledge base, and effectively navigate the complexities of the modern healthcare landscape.

The choice of pursuing additional degrees or credentials should be based on individual career goals and circumstances, considering the investment of time, energy, and money required. Employer-sponsored programs may simplify the decision-making process, but consulting colleagues, mentors, and physician leaders is essential for informed choices regarding the value and relevance of each degree or credential in the professional landscape.

REFERENCES

1. Top 35 Most Affordable Healthcare Administration Master's Degree Programs for 2023. Masters in Health Administration. HealthcareAdministration.EDU.org. https://www.healthcareadministrationedu.org/top-35-most-affordable-healthcare-administration-masters-degree-programs-for-2018-19/

2. Grover J. Masters in Public Health in USA: Top Universities, Cost & Scope. Collegedunia. April 1, 2024. https://collegedunia.com/usa/article/masters-in-public-health-in-usa-comprehensive-course-guide#

3. Courses Page | AAPL. American Association for Physician Leadership. https://www.physicianleaders.org/education/courses?

4. Hanson M. Average Cost of Law School. EducationData.org. September 13, 2023. https://educationdata.org/average-cost-of-law-school

5. Hanson M. Average Cost of a Doctorate Degree. Education Data.org. February 22, 2024. https://educationdata.org/average-cost-of-a-doctorate-degree.

6. American College of Healthcare Executives. Earn My FACHE. May 2, 2024. https://www.ache.org/fache/earn-my-fache

7. American College of Healthcare Executives. 2022 Members and Fellows Profile. ACHE. May 2, 2024. https://www.ache.org/-/media/ache/learning-center/research/2022-02-23-members-and-fellows-profile.pdf

8. Espada J. From A Financial Standpoint Is A Medical Education Worth the Investment? Med Student Money Blog. Indiana University School of Medicine. August 8, 2012. https://medicine.iu.edu/blogs/med-student-money/from-a-financial-standpoint-is-a-medical-education-worth-the-investment

9. Stoller JK, Goodall A, Baker A. Why The Best Hospitals Are Managed by Doctors. *Harvard Business Review*. December 27, 2016. https://hbr.org/2016/12/why-the-best-hospitals-are-managed-by-doctors

10. Toby Cosgrove, M.D., Announces His Decision to Transition from President, CEO Role. The Cleveland Clinic. Newsroom, May 1, 2017. https://newsroom.clevelandclinic.org/2017/05/01/toby-cosgrove-m-d-announces-decision-transition-president-ceo-role

11. U.S. Bureau of Labor Statistics. Occupational Outlook Handbook: Medical and Health Services Managers. April 17, 2024. https://www.bls.gov/ooh/management/medical-and-health-services-managers.htm

12. The White Coat Investor. MBA for Doctors. Is an MD MBA Worth It? White Coat Investor blog. January 19, 2021. https://www.whitecoatinvestor.com/is-an-mba-worth-it-for-an-md

13. Proctor C. Is an MBA Worth It for Physicians? Student Loan Planner. February 20, 2024. https://www.studentloanplanner.com/is-md-mba-physicians-worth-it/

14. Du JY, Rascoe AS, Marcus RE. The Growing Executive-Physician Wage Gap in Major US Nonprofit Hospitals and Burden of Nonclinical Workers on the US Healthcare System. *Clin Orthop Relat Res*. 2018 Oct;476(10):1910–1919. doi: 10.1097/CORR.0000000000000394.

15. Bennett D. Why Physicians Should Get an MBA. AMN Healthcare. July 10, 2023 https://www.amnhealthcare.com/blog/physician/perm/why-physicians-should-get-an-mba/#:~:text=As%20medicine%20becomes%20more%20of,just%20a%20few%20MBA%20programs

16. The 156 Most Affordable MBA Healthcare Management Online Programs. GetEducated. https://www.geteducated.com/online-college-ratings-and-rankings/mba-healthcare-management-online/#/

17. Should You Get a Healthcare MBA or an MHA? The Quantic Blog. Quantic School of Business and Technology. January 3, 2023. https://quantic.edu/blog/2023/01/03/should-you-get-a-healthcare-mba-or-an-mha/

18. What Is a Master of Healthcare Administration (MHA) Degree? University of Minnesota. School of Public Health. Health. https://www.sph.umn.edu/academics/degrees-programs/mha/degree-information/

19. Broeska H. The Healthcare Claims Adjudication Process in the United States—A Picture Is Worth A Thousand Words. ResearchGate. May 2019. https://www.researchgate.net/publication/332960120_The_healthcare_claims_adjudication_process_in_the_United_States-A_picture_is_worth_a_thousand_words

20. Number of Healthcare Administrators Is Rising. Athenahealth. https://www.athenahealth.com/knowledge-hub/practice-management/expert-forum-rise-and-rise-healthcare-administrator

21. What Is a Master of Public Health (MPH) Degree? School of Public Health - University of Minnesota School of Public Health. https://www.sph.umn.edu/academics/degrees-programs/mph/degree-information

22. Martin WF, Long HW, Culbertson RA, Beyt E. The Master of Medical Management (MMM) Degree: An Analysis of Alumni Perceptions. *J Health Adm Educ.* 2007 Fall;24(4):391–398. PMID: 18578267.

23. Conversation with Devon Glasgow of AAPL on November 7, 2023.

24. Angood P. Profiles in Success: Certified Physician Executives Share the Value and ROI of their CPE Education. White Paper. AAPL. April 2024. www.physicianleaders.org https://doi.org/10.55834/wp.8139640919

25. Jones L. Combined MD-JD Programs. US News & World Report. February 28, 2023. https://www.usnews.com/education/articles/combined-md-jd-degrees-what-to-know

26. Haskins J. Oh, the Places You'll Go with an MD (and More). Newsroom. AAMC. https://www.aamc.org/news/oh-places-you-ll-go-md-and-more

27. Dueling Degrees: Why Some Doctors Are Getting a JD. Amednews.com. January 28, 2002. https://amednews.com/article/20020128/profession/301289999/4

28. AAMD. National MD-PhD Program Outcomes Study. 2018. https://store.aamc.org/national-md-phd-program-outcomes-study.html

29. Katzowitz J. Is an MD/PhD Worth It? Financial Breakdown. White Coat Investor. 27 May 27, 2023. https://www.whitecoatinvestor.com/md-ph-d-good-financial-decision/

CHAPTER 5

Important Characteristics of a CMO Applicant

Lee S. Scheinbart, MD, CPE

EARLY IN MY CAREER, I advocated for our health system to support the local hospice with the development of a freestanding hospice house. I pushed the issue with executive leadership at every encounter until, finally, the CEO suggested that I take on the project myself. He told me that in his career, certain projects succeeded only when a physician champion got involved. He added that I was the only doctor on the medical staff who had made this an issue and that I would be a natural agent to make the hospice house a reality.

As was typical of that era, I was selected because I was passionate, relentless (if not annoying), and as an oncologist, all too familiar with the role and value of the hospice approach to patients. In other words, I was a cocky, pesky, subject-matter expert and the CEO wanted to give me something to occupy my time and turn my attention away from bugging him.

At that time, I knew nothing about project management or leadership (aside from what I learned in Boy Scouts), but to our mutual surprise, the house was built and years later the community created two more freestanding hospice houses.

About 30 years ago, it was rather typical of a CEO to select a subject-matter expert and respected physician for leadership roles, even if they did not have traditional training or experience in those roles. It was assumed that anyone who had earned their medical degree was competent enough to step into these roles. That formula has since largely been replaced by a modern executive search approach that places high value on several discrete qualities that are required in physician executive roles.

EVOLVING ROLES

As I took on roles of greater responsibility over the course of my career, including the role of chief medical officer (CMO), I witnessed the evolution of what C-suite executives seek in physician executive partners.

Just as healthcare has evolved over the last three decades, so has the role of the CMO. It began as a title endowed to a senior physician with scant executive training and few management responsibilities. With the tightening of reimbursement, the compression of margin, increasing regulations from CMS, and heightened focus on efficiency, hospital executives sought greater support from their management teams to meet the increasing complexity of operating the hospital. There was a need to place physician leaders in a more comprehensive and ever evolving roles, such as the chief medical officer.

A long time ago, at a seminar devoted to aspiring physician executives, the lead faculty speaker asked his class of students, "What does VPMA stand for?" and several physicians promptly shouted, "vice president of medical affairs," to which the lecturer replied, "No! It means Fix the Docs!"

He went on to say that when hospital CEOs seek to have a VPMA or CMO on their executive team, they want a leader who can herd the cats, as the expression goes. And, in fact, years ago, there was a generally accepted truth that the primary function of the VPMA/CMO was simply to work with the chief of staff/president of the medical staff, the Medical Executive Committee, the department chairs, and the entire medical staff to ensure that there was adherence to the medical staff bylaws, rules and regulations, and policies. Further, the CEO often sought a seasoned physician with a solid reputation and an ability to butt heads with the medical staff as the two main pre-requisites for the role of VPMA/CMO.

Over time, however, hospitals underwent several changes, including acquisition by larger hospital chains, acquisition of physician groups, and vertical integrations of significant scale, inclusive of health insurance plans. This not only changed the role and responsibilities of the CEO, but it also refined the CMO role.[1] In fact, each of these individual health system components would ultimately need CMOs, while in some cases, the emerging systems elevated individuals into roles of chief clinical officer or chief physician executive to oversee the various components (e.g., hospitals, medical groups, health plan, urgent care, etc.) each of which had a CMO.

IMPORTANT CHARACTERISTICS

This brings us to the current landscape wherein CEOs/COOs seek a variety of qualities and skills when recruiting and/or elevating physician executives into any number of CMO roles. A recent, informal survey of chief executives conducted by this book's editors identified several important characteristics that they seek when evaluating CMO candidates. These characteristics are listed, in alphabetical order, in Table 1. When reviewing this list for your purposes, however, it may be more pragmatic if the components were put under one of two frameworks for either a CEO or a CMO to utilize.

TABLE 1. Characteristics Sought by Chief Executives When Hiring a CMO

Articulate
Communicator
Compassion
Connector
Does Not Talk Down to Physicians
Focus on Quality
Honesty
Influential
Integrity
(Servant) Leader
Listener
Not Manipulative
Positive Attitude
Relationship Builder

The first framework derives from Patrick Lencioni's book *The Ideal Team Player*.[2] Lencioni suggests three indispensable virtues that a CEO ought to look for when hiring an executive to join the team:

The first of these virtues is "Humble." As described in the book, a candidate should lack an excessive ego and concern for status. This is best embodied by the ability to quickly point out the contributions of others while slowly seeking recognition for their own contribution. The credit for success is shared and the collective results are greater than the individual parts.

The second trait is "Hungry." A candidate should always look for more responsibility and more knowledge. The candidate is naturally self-motivated and diligent in their efforts and productivity. They are constantly thinking about the next step or the next opportunity.

The third trait is "Smart." Particularly "People Smart." This requires the candidate to display a high degree of emotional intelligence when it comes to other people. In other words, the candidate should have a good deal of common sense about people and have a keen sense of situational awareness in a group setting. The candidate uses good judgment and intuition when dealing with others and knows the difference between the intent and the impact of their words and actions. With these three virtues we can organize our list of characteristics into an easier to remember framework (see Table 2).

TABLE 2. Framework of Virtues

Humble	Hungry	(People) Smart
Compassion	Be Positive (Attitude)	Articulate
Honesty	Communicator	Don't Talk Down to Physicians
Integrity	Connector	Influential
(Servant) Leader	Focus (on Quality)	Not manipulative
Listener		Relationship Builder

On the other hand, the Lencioni triad does not cover all the items listed in the informal survey. For that, we can develop a second framework that is more binary with one column holding a To Do list and the other containing a Do Not Do list (see Table 3). This framing encourages positive contributions on the one hand and serves as a reminder or a proverbial stop sign to check actions that are negatively received.

TABLE 3. To Do and Not-to-Do List

To Do	Not To Do
(Be a Servant) Leader	(Fail to) Articulate
Build Relationships	Be Manipulative
Compassion	Be Negative
Focus on Quality	(Fail to) Communicate
Influence	(Fail to) Connect
Integrity	(Fail to be) Honest
Listen	Talk Down To Physicians

The To Do list fosters growth for the individual and helps them model behaviors that strengthen the organizational culture. The Do Not Do list contains derailing conduct that will undermine the mission of the organization and achievement of its goals.

TRUST AND INFLUENCE

Regardless of the framing, let's take a moment to look more closely at just a few characteristics identified in the survey (Table 1) that stand out both individually and collectively. These include *active listening, open communication*, and *humility* and are critical elements in creating psychological safety among teams in organizations.

In healthcare, Amy Edmonson researched the value of psychological safety (which was subsequently supported by Project Aristotle), as a means of understanding the relationship between error making and teamwork in hospitals.[3,4] Not surprisingly, teams that shared enhanced psychological safety were more effective in catching errors and improving safety and quality.

All healthcare executives must maintain vigilance in their operations to reduce errors and improve outcomes for patients; CEOs will depend on CMOs to be the chief stewards of quality and safety, such that these traits will be highly valued by the hiring CEO. Additionally, these elements, along with the display of *integrity*, not only facilitate the creation of psychological safety, but they also engender *trust*.[5]

With trust comes the role of *influence*, perhaps the single most-desired skill sought by CEOs when considering a CMO for hire. The CMO's position alone, even if they are the highest-ranking physician in an organization, "will not engage physicians, nor will likability or popularity suffice."[5] To engage physicians, the CMO "must be able to leverage influence."[5]

Regardless of the number of direct reports, operational responsibilities, budget items, and authority given to the CMO, the chief physician must master the use of *influence* to inspire other physicians to action. Although CMOs have gradually obtained more organizational control in the past decade, especially with the COVID-19 pandemic, the CMO should try to have even greater influence than control in order to widen their effectiveness.

Influence is the persuasive skill of getting people to say "yes" and what moves people to change behavior, both of which are highly desirable in the world of organizational effectiveness.[6] These specific elements, when combined, are likely the ones most highly sought by CEOs, as these are recognized as critical to moving large components of the hospital or clinic or system to the desired organizational goals of safety, quality, and the delivery of care (see Figure 1).

FIGURE 1. Characteristics of an Effective Organizational Leader

SELF-EVALUATION

As you consider advancing your career, conduct a valid "360" self-evaluation relative to the lists of characteristics in this chapter. For example, write down each of the 15 traits listed in Table 1 and self-rate them (1 to 10 scale) as displaying the trait poorly (1) or exceptionally well (10). Then ask 3–4 important people in your life (spouse/partner/best friend, co-worker/peer, nurse leader/non-clinical director, current boss) to conduct an honest rating of you using the same scale on the same traits.

With the results in hand, ask yourself if you are the same person in their eyes that you see in the mirror. Challenge yourself to close any gaps in the way you see yourself and how others perceive you. Have one-on-ones with those individuals and solicit genuine, honest feedback and examples that highlight any of your lower-scoring attributes.

While you should not include the results of this assignment on your resume, you should not disregard the value of the exercise to your personal development; it may serve you well should a question or two pop up in your interview that asks you to define your weaknesses or areas under development.

Once you have concluded the inspection of your own skill set relative to what is sought by the hiring executive, consider the following "next steps." If you presently have access to a leadership development program (or simply a leadership skills coach), sign up for the program. Many, if not all, of the characteristics discussed in this chapter are also connected to leadership. As a construct, "leadership requires the modeling of desired behaviors, the exhibition of required skills, the techniques used to inspire action, and an understanding of the environment."[7]

The overlap here is not coincidental; CEOs may not be looking only for a discrete set of attributes in a CMO, but also for a leader. By spending the requisite time on developing these skills, you are investing in your success as an executive.

In addition to honing leadership skills, consider attending a CMO academy. These programs focus on the discrete elements that are linked to the job duties of the CMO, such as clinical value proposition, healthcare finance, regulatory/legal issues, quality/safety/risk, population health, etc.

Even if you don't yet have the experience, if you learn basic working knowledge of the key issues facing healthcare executives today, it telegraphs to the hiring CEO that you are serious about taking on the role and the responsibilities of CMO. If you show your humility by attending leadership courses and if you show you are hungry to learn about the CMO role, you will be way ahead of the curve compared to other candidates for the role.

Finally, if you are fortunate enough to be considered for a role, perform the following litmus tests before accepting any offer. First, ask for the opportunity to have an executive coach during the first 90–180 days in your new role. It will (again!) speak highly of your humility and hunger to learn.

Second, be wary if your future boss (and/or your future organization) is dismissive of executive coaching or shows no interest or familiarity in the construct of "Humble, Hungry, Smart" attributes when seeking an ideal team player. If you are sensing strong resistance to fostering your career, you may want to re-consider your pursuit of the role at the institution where you are interviewing. The reactions to these elements of the offer say much more about the organization you are about to lead than you may realize.

While individual talents are critically important to succeed as a CMO, in order to be set up for success, the organization ought to support the role and be willing to invest in it, lest you become relegated to outdated thinking and forever tasked to "Fix the Docs!"

KEEP IT SIMPLE

In closing, I must express my gratitude to the hospital CEO who selected me to champion the cause of the hospice house. With many years of experience behind me and with the ability to now look back at that time in my career, I can only hope that he saw characteristics in me that I did not see in myself. By placing a certain degree of responsibility in my hands and by allowing me to shepherd the project (all the while I imagine he must have kept a close eye on me), I learned quite a bit about my own arrogance, my own sense of urgency, and my failure to know the environment.

I now understand that VPMA is better translated as "*Lead* the Docs," and that a CMO must be a team player. After attending CMO readiness courses, receiving leadership development, and experiencing executive coaching, I can attest to their value and how much can be accomplished by distilling things down to simple advice.

Of course, as Carl Jung said, "…this sounds very simple, but simple things are always the most difficult. In actual life it requires the greatest discipline to be simple, and the acceptance of oneself is the essence of the moral problem and the epitome of a whole outlook upon life."[8] And, if all else fails while preparing your personal characteristics for the role of CMO, remember this piece of simple advice, first stated by St. Francis of Assisi in the 13th century and later re-phrased by Steven Covey, the author of *The 7 Habits of Highly Effective People*: "Seek first to understand, then to be understood."[9]

REFERENCES

1. Hlavin J. CMO Experiences: A Rudimentary Case Report. *Physicians Leadership Journal*. 2019;6(5):43–49.

2. Lencioni P. *The Ideal Team Player: How to Recognize and Cultivate The Three Essential Virtues*. Hoboken, NJ: Jossey-Bass; 2016.

3. Edmondson A. *The Fearless Organization: Creating Psychological Safety in the Workplace for Learning, Innovation, and Growth*. Hoboken, NJ: John Wiley & Sons; 2018.

4. Charles D. What Google Learned From Its Quest to Build the Perfect Team. *New York Times*. Feb. 25, 2016. https://www.nytimes.com/2016/02/28/magazine/what-google-learned-from-its-quest-to-build-the-perfect-team.html

5. Sonnenberg M. Chief Medical Officer: Changing Roles and Skill Sets for Chief Medical Officers. *Physician Leadership Journal*. 2015;2(1):16–21.

6. Cialdini RB. *Influence: Science and Practice (4th ed.)*. Boston, MA: Allyn and Bacon; 2001.

7. Hertling M. Lt. Gen, US Army (Ret.) Personal quote.

8. Jung C. *Psychology and Religion; West and East*. New York, NY: Pantheon Books; 1958.

9. Covey S. *The 7 Habits of Highly Effective People*. New York, NY: Free Press; 2004.

PART III

Applying for the Job

CHAPTER 6

So, You Want to Be a Chief Medical Officer: Landing the Right Job

Michele L. Arnold, MD, MBA

"**D**R. ARNOLD, HAVE YOU EVER thought about being a *physician executive*?" he asked.

I was a few years out of residency, starting a family and establishing a clinical practice in my first "real job." Yet, I found myself sitting in the office of our hospital CEO, who was asking me a pivotal question.

Dr. Todd Sorensen was an internist and an introvert, gifted with the mind of an engineer. He was the highly respected and pensive leader of our organization and a pillar of the community and region, recognized and trusted by all.

I recall examining his face as he asked me this question. Wrinkles on the left outnumbered those on the right but seemed to perfectly align when he perched his chin in a thoughtful left hand. I surmised he adopted that posture often, and for long hours.

"Excuse me, *a what*?" I postulated naively. I squinted at the binary clock on his desk, trying to decipher its code. He took note.

At the time, I didn't know what he saw in me, nor what paths were ahead of me. But as I reflect, that moment was undoubtedly my calling to physician leadership.

Perhaps you've heard a leadership call of your own, and you are ready to respond. Or perhaps like many physician leaders, you've been swept upward into leadership in a frenzy, as if storming a beach in a war zone, and when you look around, you astonishingly realize you're in command.

No matter where you are in your physician leadership journey, *now* is the perfect time to stop and take inventory of your current role and **decide who/where you want to be in 3–5 years**. Why? (Also, this is a favorite interview question.) While clinical physician roles often grow into a multi-decade legacy, most other industry leaders occupy a given role/title for 3–5 years, then move into another.

Stepping off the clinical treadmill and into leadership welcomes a different trajectory and timeline for growth and advancement. Without a clear strategy and tactical plan, it can be easy to get lost or swept up the beach.

In this chapter, I hope to guide you through nine steps of a successful CMO job search, based on recent personal experience in this space. The job search process can be, at best, unfamiliar and curious, and at worst, painful and demoralizing. Regardless, the entire process is a growth opportunity, and I recommend taking these steps in the order listed.

STEP 1: DEFINE YOUR IDEAL LEADERSHIP ROLE.

The many options for physician leadership are staggering (see Table 1). Without a doubt, the first (and possibly most challenging) step is to decide what type of position you want. When you don't really know what you want, a recruiter will have a difficult time matching you to a role.

Take some time to learn about the different roles, what they involve, and what skills, gifts, prerequisites, degrees, and credentials are required. To be well-equipped, physicians often need additional training in business, informatics, operations, process improvement, strategy, people management, medical staff bylaws, negotiation, finance, legal, governance, and leadership.

Physicians choose their specialty based as much on what they love as what they *don't* love. Every specialty has its blemishes, and similarly, every executive role has its burdens. Some roles may require overnight administrative call coverage, while others expect bankers' hours. For some roles, there may be the implication of being "always on," 24/7/365. Some allow the physician executive to maintain a small clinical practice while others don't. Some have community obligations or responsibilities to a board of directors.

Moreover, determine what a typical day looks like in each of these roles. How much of your day will you spend in meetings, rounding, doing chart review, interviewing applicants, developing policy, negotiating contracts, developing compensation models, or doing performance reviews? Will you be coaching medical staff and employees, or will you be holding them

TABLE 1. A Few Physician Executive Roles

Program Director
Medical Director
Executive (Senior) Medical Director
Regional Medical Director
Service Line Director
Institute/Clinical Program Director
Vice President Medical Affairs (VPMA)
Chief Medical Officer (CMO)
Chief Quality Officer (CQO)
Chief Safety Officer (CSO)
Chief Medical Informatics Officer (CMIO)
Chief Information Officer (CIO)
Chief Experience Officer (CXO)
Chief People Officer
Chief Health Equity Officer
Chief Strategy Officer (CSO)
Chief Clinical Officer
Chief Operations Officer (COO)
Chief Executive Officer (CEO)

accountable for misconduct and implementing performance improvement plans? Will you be developing best practice initiatives, or will you be implementing them? Will you get a data analyst assigned to you, or will *you* be the data analyst?

I recommend interviewing or shadowing a few colleagues in these various roles to get a glimpse of the good, the bad, and the ugly of each job.

STEP 2: DEFINE YOUR IDEAL INDUSTRY AND CULTURE.

As medical students and residents, we get acquainted with several healthcare work settings, but the possibilities for physician leadership expand far beyond what you will experience in training (see Table 2). Many of the roles listed in Table 1 exist within the settings listed in Table 2.

When discerning the various work settings, consider your personal values vis-à-vis the values of the organization. While patient care remains central,

TABLE 2. Physician Executive Work Settings

• Hospital (community hospital, regional referral center, tertiary, quaternary, rural/critical access hospital, VA, not-for-profit, for-profit, behavioral health facility) • Post-acute care (IRF, SNF, LTAC, NH, home health) • Employed medical group • Private practice group • National private practice physician group (i.e., corporate medicine) • Locum/staffing agency • Governmental agency – state, federal, and international orgs for quality (AHRQ, NCQA, NQF, IHI), hospitals (AHA), even CMS and state Medicaid entities • Insurance company – these roles largely revolve around peer review and utilization review and oversight thereof • Pharmaceutical • ACGME (e.g., residency program director)
Other non-clinical roles:
• Faculty (medical school, undergraduate) • Utilization management • Executive coaching • Various types of consulting roles • TJC or DNV surveyor • Tech start-ups • DME/medical device vendors

the mission, biases, and interests can differ substantially between hospital, ambulatory, government, pharma, and payer organizations.

For example, workplace culture in a not-for-profit environment may focus on sustainability and stewardship of limited resources, whereas a for-profit insurance mogul may prioritize financial performance and shareholder earnings. Moreover, physicians themselves may be viewed through a different lens in these various settings.

Compensation and employee benefits vary widely; non-profits may offer opportunities for loan repayment or tuition assistance, while for-profits offer stock options and government roles may offer pensions. Longevity and security differ across the spectrum as well; check your level of risk-aversity when considering an entrepreneurial or tech start-up opportunity.

STEP 3: IDENTIFY YOUR IDEAL GEOGRAPHY.

"Location, location, location" is a ubiquitous real estate mantra, repeated thrice to prevent overlooking the importance of location as a primary driver of valuation. As you consider your job opportunities, ask whether *this* is a place where you and your loved ones can live and thrive. Most recruiters limit their search and ad distributions by geography. Some regional leadership roles require frequent travel, while others permit work from home. You may wish to consider this as you seek your next position.

The other side of the coin, however, is that physicians who hold leadership positions in larger multi-state organizations *and are willing to relocate* may be offered more opportunities to advance.

STEP 4: GET ACQUAINTED WITH YOUR LEADERSHIP SKILLS AND GIFTS.

Once you've outlined your wants, turn your attention to what you have to offer. You are likely to be among many other high achievers being considered for any given role. What are the unique experiences, learnings, behaviors, habits, values, and attributes that make you an ideal candidate for the role you seek?

A brief note on branding, differentiators, values, and 360s: During a recent job search, I benefitted immensely from leadership exercises focusing on developing my professional/leadership "brand." Authentically weaving together my own purpose, mission, values, and innate personality attributes, I was able to identify what truly differentiates me as a leader, and hence, the benefits I personally add to a role.

For me, branding has become a lifelong process of refining my personal mantra — one that defines me and continues to be redefined *by* me. Often development of a personal brand follows the exercise of defining your professional values — the beliefs and principles that guide your life and work. If you've never explored this, short Harvard Business Review articles by Cozma and Smallwood can get you acquainted with both concepts.[1,2]

Additionally, I strongly recommend submitting to a 360-degree evaluation process in your current job. Anonymous feedback from your reports, colleagues, and superiors often reveals eye-opening truths about how others see your strengths and weaknesses. Humility and self-awareness remain invaluable leadership characteristics.

STEP 5: SPIFF UP YOUR CV.

An executive CV often looks strikingly different from a clinical CV. As physicians climb the hierarchy that is medical education, we collect a litany of accolades: academic achievements, board certifications, publications, invited lectures, volunteer activities, awards and acknowledgments, and the like. Having recruited many physicians and physician leaders, I've seen CVs extend more than 50 pages, like an autobiographical soliloquy. Thus far, I've never met a COO or CEO who read the entire thing, no matter how epic. Longer is *not* better.

I recommend customizing your CV to the role you seek, condensing irrelevant sections or removing them entirely (e.g., lectures and publications upon request or placed in addenda). In fact, consider having different CVs for distinct roles.

Most executive CVs begin with a short paragraph of prose highlighting elements of your brand and what differentiates you, like an "elevator pitch." In the sections that follow, include your prior leadership experience and titles, but succinctly outline the business accomplishments you achieved in those prior roles. Where possible, quantify (in dollars) the value each project added to the organization. If you held other leadership positions (department or committee chair, leadership in a professional organization), highlight any achievements or projects you led as part of that role.

When listing references, consider separating clinical colleagues (e.g., a department chair, a favorite consultant, a lead investigator, faculty, or a collaborator from your specialty's professional association) from professional contacts (e.g., administrative dyads, and operational or strategic leaders like COOs and CEOs). Fellow clinicians affirm your clinical skills and judgment; professional references attest to your character and your leadership acumen. You might have different references based on each role you are applying for, leveraging any potential connections between your references and your potential interviewers.

One question often surfaces: cover letter or not? I favor a cover letter, since it gives you an opportunity to demonstrate your skill in writing a concise executive summary. If you intend to include a cover letter, be succinct and make it personal. A few paragraphs should suffice and should include reasons why you are seeking this role and what you could bring to it.

Use good judgment when deciding whether to list your personal or business contact information on your CV. Nothing rattles your current employer like calls from a recruiter or worse, a rival organization. I recommend a robust LinkedIn profile that is reflective of you and your brand.

It should also go without saying that any and all online and social media representations of you should reflect your character and values. They are discoverable and do contribute to hiring decisions.

STEP 6: LAUNCH THE JOB SEARCH.

Without a doubt, the search for a physician executive role starts with networking, both inside and outside of your current professional circles. When making connections, cast a wide net. Often your first and best opportunities lie within these circles of influence.

Connect with your company's internal recruiter and express your desire for internal advancement and leadership opportunities. Your recruiter can keep you informed of internal positions before they are posted, as well as any opportunities available for nomination. Many executive roles are filled with an able and willing interim who earns their keep through on-the-job successes.

If you are seeking an organizational, geographic, or industry shake-up, you will begin a legitimate job search. For a concierge experience, partner with an executive search firm like Korn-Ferry, Witt-Kieffer, B.E. Smith, or many others. (For additional resources, Hunt Scanlon Media publishes an annual listing of the top 50 healthcare executive search firms that is available online at https://huntscanlon.com/top-50/.)

Most larger organizations have their own internal recruiters who are open to being contracted directly, in the event you are targeting a specific organization. Specialty-specific recruiters can connect you with leadership opportunities within your medical specialty or within a specialty facility (e.g., dialysis facility, rehab facility, etc.).

Beyond recruiters, the job search involves hitting the virtual pavement: online job boards. Most opportunities are posted online (even executive opportunities!), and you'll need to channel your inner archeologist by doing some meticulous digging and frequent sifting. Some opportunities will be cross posted on multiple sites, while others may only be posted for 3-5 days before they close. (One small caveat: Most industries outside of healthcare recognize CMO as chief marketing officer, so search carefully.)

Online job postings can be found on large employers' websites, professional association websites, Indeed.com, LinkedIn.com, Doximity.

com, American Association for Physician Leadership (https://jobsearch. physicianleaders.org/jobs/), American College of Healthcare Executives (https://www.ache.org/career-resource-center), ExecThread (https:// execthread.com/), GlassDoor.com, and even Monster.com and more.

If you time it right, annual assemblies or specialty society meetings often have in-person job fairs, booths, or expos with posted opportunities and even onsite screening interviews.

Once you begin the process, commit to frequently checking your email, voice mail, and direct messages (e.g., LinkedIn, Doximity) for leads. Looking for a position can admittedly feel like a part-time job, but diligence and timeliness pay dividends.

STEP 7: PREPARE FOR THE SELECTION PROCESS AND INTERVIEW.

Most employers follow a detailed hiring process for candidate selection — one that begins with winnowing. Your CV, cover letter (when appropriate), and online application are filtered through an algorithm that chooses only those candidates who meet certain selection criteria.

You may be required to upload your CV, then regurgitate salient information from your CV into an online form. Each employer may have a different format, and the process can become redundant and monotonous. (I suspect this is some form of divine payback for the multiple forms we require of patients in clinical settings.) A complete application and a high tolerance for tedium are required to be part of the wheat, as opposed to the chaff.

Once you pass the winnowing round, you likely will be contacted via email or phone to arrange a one-on-one call with a hiring manager or executive. This "scout call" is your first live encounter with a potential employer, and a chance to get a feel for fit, not unlike a blind date.

They've undoubtedly researched you, and it is important that you do some research on that person, as well. If the scout call goes well, a virtual one-on-one or panel interview is likely to follow. Do your prep work and know the organization, your interviewers, and their roles.

Finally, an onsite interview is among the final steps. At this phase, you are likely one of two or three final candidates. Be prepared to answer detailed questions from your CV, typically focused on your past successes and failures. Anticipate questions that begin with "tell me about a time when … ."

Be prepared to speak candidly about your weaknesses and what you've learned from your failures. Share examples of interpersonal conflicts you've navigated or rifts you've mended and speak about your past contributions. Speak about how you would provide a return on investment.

This is the time to pull from your personal leadership brand: Let your differentiators shine, show how your actions reflect your values, and don't forget to demonstrate humility and self-awareness. As you speak your values, note in particular how they align with your potential employer's. Compose several thoughtful questions for your interviewers — don't forget that *you are interviewing them* as much as they are interviewing you. Be succinct, using care not to dominate the conversation; allow for banter.

Additionally, let it be known that there is *never* a moment during the interview process when you are not "on stage." The way you treat travel schedulers, executive assistants, recruiters, restaurant staff, real estate agents, and front desk and back office personnel *matters*, and often gets back to hiring managers.

STEP 8: MAKE DECISIONS.

Chances are, you'll go through many rounds of interviews with many organizations. On my most recent relocation, I was exploring nine different opportunities and traveled across four different time zones. How do you keep them all straight? How do you decide among many different offers?

I benefitted greatly from keeping a detailed spreadsheet delineating each role, the facility/organization, location, any/all contacts, and a status update for where in the process I was. As I traveled the interview circuit, I ranked each role along numerous criteria (outlined in Table 3).

(Side note: I freely admit I nerded out and got very granular, attributing a comparable numeric value to every factor within each domain in Table 3, according to how much I personally value that item, whether monumental [e.g., compensation] or frivolous [e.g., office aesthetics]. I then designed a formula that took the weighted average and helped me rank the positions. There was no overthinking or double-guessing, and it was a game-changer for me and my family. For example: I value a bright, inspiring work

TABLE 3. Factors to Consider

ORGANIZATIONAL FACTORS
  People: Culture mission
  People: Local team
  People: Regional team
  Politics/Gaming
  My risk
  Financial sustainability

DESTINATION FACTORS
  Place: Beauty
  Place: Climate
  Place: Amenities (shopping, theater, music, sports)
  Place: Accessibility (airport, proximity to loved ones)
  Place: Vibe
  Aesthetics: Campus
  Aesthetics: My office

FAMILY FACTORS
  Spouse
  Child #1
  Child #2 (and so on)
  Extended family

PROFESSIONAL FACTORS
  Professional development
  Compensation
  Advancement opportunities
  Benefits
  Vacation/Paid time off
  After-hours responsibilities

COMMUNITY FACTORS
  Neighborhood
  School
  Places of worship
  Housing: Quality, availability
  Housing: Cost

COMPENSATION FACTORS
  Compensation base
  Cost of living adjustment (vs. current location)
  Compensation incentive
  Compensation extras

Weighted average of each = TOTAL SCORE

environment, and hence, I weighted "office aesthetics" accordingly. I passed on one potential opportunity because the physician office itself was the size of a European hotel room and lined with 1970s wood-paneling = zero points for office aesthetics.)

STEP 9: NEGOTIATE.

Assigning relative values to the factors in Table 3 also informs your negotiations. Online cost-of-living calculators can be applied to compensation in various locations to enable salary parity. Additionally, trade-offs in one area may help you leverage your negotiations for non-comp perks like professional development opportunities, a signing bonus, reimbursement for relocation expenses, permission to maintain a small clinical FTE, or even exclusion from the administrative call pool. Salary aside, there are many ways to carve a role to your benefit.

One caveat: Employment contracts are not a universal entity across executive roles. Ideally, a signed contract provides employees with certain protections (e.g., duty to give notice, protections against arbitrary termination, etc.). If you favor security, or feel the pros outweigh the cons (e.g., non-compete clause, claims to intellectual property), consider requesting a contract.

AS YOU EMBARK ON YOUR JOURNEY

In 2007, author Gene Weingarten published in *The Washington Post* an article about a social experiment known as the Great Subway Station Violin Experiment.[3,4] World-famous violin virtuoso Joshua Bell played a $3.5 million Stradivari violin in the arcade of D.C.'s L'Enfant Plaza subway station for 43 minutes, managing to gather a few onlookers, thunderous silence, and $32.17 in tips. Days before, he had sold out Boston's Symphony Hall at $100 per ticket.

The experiment begs the question, "In a banal setting at an inconvenient time, would beauty transcend?"[3] Weingarten claims we "shouldn't be too ready to label the Metro passersby as unsophisticated boobs. Context matters."[3]

I believe the larger answer is exemplified by this oft-repeated quote: "The extraordinary in an ordinary environment does not shine and is so often overlooked and undervalued." Know your worth and seek for yourself an environment that not only values you but serves and rewards you accordingly.

REFERENCES

1. Cozma I. How to Find, Define, and Use Your Values. *Harvard Business Review.* February 7, 2023. https://hbr.org/2023/02/how-to-find-define-and-use-your-values.

2. Smallwood N. Define Your Personal Leadership Brand in Five Steps. *Harvard Business Review.* March 29, 2010. https://hbr.org/2010/03/define-your-personal-leadershi.

3. Weingarten G. Pearls Before Breakfast: Can One of the Nation's Great Musicians Cut Through the Fog of a D.C. Rush Hour? Let's Find Out. *The Washington Post.* April 8, 2007. https://www.washingtonpost.com/lifestyle/magazine/pearls-before-breakfast-can-one-of-the-nations-great-musicians-cut-through-the-fog-of-a-dc-rush-hour-lets-find-out/2014/09/23/8a6d46da-4331-11e4-b47c-f5889e061e5f_story.html.

4. Weingarten G. Setting the Record Straight on the Joshua Bell Experiment. *The Washington Post.* October 14, 2014. https://www.washingtonpost.com/news/style/wp/2014/10/14/gene-weingarten-setting-the-record-straight-on-the-joshua-bell-experiment/?utm_term=.c2d2483a2052.

CHAPTER 7

How to Assess a Specific Chief Medical Officer Job

Steven D. Brass, MD, MPH, MBA, FACHE

WHEN DETERMINING WHETHER A CHIEF medical officer job is a good fit, there are several items that should be on your checklist to consider. The priority of each of these items is up to the individual job seeker to determine before making the final decision whether to take on a new job.

- Motivation for seeking a new position/reason for leaving the current position.
- Job description of the new position in relation to your current qualifications.
- Results of due diligence around the health system, hospital, and executive team.
- Compensation.
- Work-life balance.
- Organizational culture.
- Personal goals and professional growth opportunities.
- Leadership dynamics.

Use the checklist to create notes as you begin to evaluate the position. Discuss the positives and negatives of a potential opportunity with a mentor to verify and validate your perspective. In addition, don't ignore your internal voice or "gut feeling" about whether the job is right for you.

SELF-REFLECT ABOUT YOUR MOTIVATION.

"Find out what you like doing best and get someone to pay you for doing it." — Katharine Whitehorn

Before even looking at a job description, it is important to self-reflect on why you are looking for a chief medical officer position. What is your motivation? Are you passionate about leadership, the business side of medicine, quality, safety, and engaging in complex and oftentimes challenging conversations with other physicians and administrators while making a difference in the lives of many patients?

Or, are you leaving your current job due to burnout or job dissatisfaction? It is important to recognize that every job presents challenges, barriers, and opportunities — it's about your ability to adapt that is crucial to how you function in the job.

Think about your current qualifications and the strengths that you bring to the job: Do you have the required board certifications and state licenses? What about leadership experience, regulatory knowledge, public speaking, negotiation, and conflict-management skills?

Most importantly, what experience do you have leading change in an organization or team? It is sometimes helpful to document in writing your experience under each of these areas as you look through different job postings and prepare for interviews.

You must understand your own limitations and whether you will be able to effectively manage a large academic medical center or a smaller local community hospital. It will be more challenging for a physician from a non-academic private practice background to come into a new academic medical center as a chief medical officer without having a strong academic, research, or educational background in your back pocket.

DISSECT THE JOB DESCRIPTION WITH RESPECT TO QUALIFICATIONS NEEDED.

"Your qualifications and experiences are not merely lines on a resume; they are the chapters and verses that narrate your professional story."
— *Author Unknown*

I cannot emphasize enough the importance of thoroughly reviewing the job description so you understand exactly what the employer is looking for and, if possible, why the job is open at this time. Consider doing a gap analysis between the qualifications posted and your own qualifications to ensure alignment and potential fit.

Are they looking for a chief medical officer to take on value-based care, population health, ambulatory, correctional health, or physician alignment? Or are their "pain points" related to other quality or financial metrics?

Are they looking for someone with strong system experience managing a multi-hospital system? Or are they looking for someone who is going to be more "boots on the ground," engaging with community physicians in the doctor's lounge?

Having that understanding is important to ensure that your qualifications meet the requirements of the job. For example, you would not want to start looking for a chief medical officer job that involves a heavy population health angle without having population health knowledge/experience. Based on your qualifications and experience, are you more confident as a chief medical officer for a 75-bed rural hospital or an 800-bed large academic quaternary hospital?

RESEARCH THE HOSPITAL/ HEALTH SYSTEM IN DETAIL.

"Trust but verify." — Ronald Reagan

This quote encapsulates the idea of having confidence in others but also ensuring that the information or promises made are validated for authenticity. It is critical that you do research on the hospital, the executive team, and the larger parent company. Understand the mission, vision, and values of the company as well as the financial status of the larger health system.

- What is their strategic plan?
- How long have the executives been in place?
- Are there any changes going on at the parent company that may impact this hospital, like mergers, acquisitions, or restructuring?
- Have they recently undergone a reduction in force? Why is this position open now?
- How long has the prior CMO been in the position? Is there a large or frequent turnover in the executive team?
- Are there any new or large capital projects on the horizon that you will be involved with and that may be part of your future portfolio?
- What is the organization's current Leapfrog Grade or CMS Star Rating? Have there been any recent CMS audits, OIG audits, or state, county, or city health department audits that may help you understand their current pain points?

Having all this information will make you a stronger job candidate and interviewee. Much of it can be gleaned from the interview and through online research. I suggest doing a search of Becker's Healthcare blogs and local newspapers for any headlines that can serve as sources of information. I also suggest reviewing the publicly available 990 tax forms (not-for-profit hospital filings) to better understand the financial health of the company you are considering joining.

CONSIDER THE COMPENSATION.

"Never work just for money or for power. They won't save your soul or help you sleep at night." — Marian Wright Edelman

The compensation details of the position often are not revealed until later in the negotiations or interviews. Some state laws mandate that the salary be reported in the job description to create greater transparency and to ensure equity.

Remember that compensation includes bonuses, benefits, stock options, personal time off/vacation time, and continuing medical education allowances. Salary can often be negotiated, but do not let the salary be the only driving factor for deciding whether this job is a good fit or not. Sometimes taking a job with a lower salary may still be an amazing professional opportunity.

To determine whether the compensation offered is in keeping with the market, reference the *American College of Healthcare Executive Journal,* which publishes annual salary surveys for executives based on the organizational size. Another area that you may want to clarify is the bonus structure. What are the key performance indicators that you will be judged on to receive the bonus?

CONSIDER THE WORK/LIFE BALANCE.

"Never get so busy making a living that you forget to make a life."
— Dolly Parton

Understanding the details of what the job requires will give you a window into what kind of work/life balance is possible. Some jobs require long hours, weekend and holiday on-call responsibilities, and early morning or evening meetings. (Monthly 5 a.m. and 6 p.m. medical staff department meetings were regular occurrences at one of my organizations.) It's important to get the full picture before accepting the position, given your current social or family responsibilities may soon become competing priorities.

One litmus test question is how vacations are handled among the executive team. Are vacations encouraged? When you are on vacation are you truly on vacation or is there an unwritten expectation that you will answer your work emails and calls while on vacation?

Since the COVID-19 pandemic, meetings have been done routinely via Webex or Zoom. However, as a member of the executive team, you will be expected to have daily face-to-face time with your executive team, the physicians, your direct reports, and other members of the health system. The true work/life balance picture may not be evident until you are in the job, but this is something to consider as you take on any new position.

BECOME FAMILIAR WITH THE ORGANIZATIONAL CULTURE.

"Culture eats strategy for breakfast." — Peter Drucker

Organizational culture, also called company culture, has been defined as "the shared values, goals, attitudes, and practices that characterize a workplace. It is reflected in how people behave, interact with each other, make decisions, and do their work."[1] A strong company culture is more relevant in shaping an organization's success than even the most well-thought-out strategies. An organization's culture affects performance, employee satisfaction, and employee turnover.[2,3]

It is difficult to assess culture in the organization until you are in place. Then you can better determine how the executive team members interact with each other.

- Do the executive team members speak positively about each other or negatively behind the scenes?
- Does the team socialize outside of work hours?
- Does the executive team discuss the positive aspects of the organization or do they focus on only the negative aspects?

- How are decisions made and communicated? Is it top down or collaborative?
- What is the organizational structure like? Are there multiple levels of managers and committees making it difficult to move decisions forward?
- Are "just and accountable culture principles" used when addressing failures?
- What motivates the employees to stay in their position long term? What is the company turnover?

Your ability to accept the culture and assimilate can make or break you as a future leader in the organization and determine whether you will have a successful next step in your career.[2,3]

REFLECT ON PERSONAL GOALS AND PROFESSIONAL GROWTH.

"Train people well enough so they can leave, treat them well enough so they don't want to." — *Richard Branson*

When deliberating about the job, it is also important to consider whether your personal and professional goals are aligned. Are you looking to stay in a role for the next 10 years or are you jockeying to move up the corporate ladder? Do you fear being laid off?

Understand that every job has challenges and the average chief medical officer position spans 3–5 years. Often the CEO leaves the organization, and the new CEO recruits their own replacement executive team. Healthcare mergers and acquisitions, restructuring, reductions in force due to economic pressures also play a role in organizational culture, job stability, and your ability to grow in the organization.

- Will there be opportunities to grow and advance over time?
- Are there regional or system opportunities to grow into or will you be content staying as CMO in this local 100-bed hospital for the next 5–10 years?
- Does the organization encourage growth and development through leadership development or executive coaching?
- Have there been any recent promotions in the organization?

- Do they recruit externally or internally for new roles?
- Are there opportunities in your role to interact with the regional or system head office?
- Are there opportunities to work across the organization and make a lateral move if needed?

All these questions are important to consider when deciding whether this job is for you.

EVALUATE THE LEADERSHIP DYNAMICS.

"The way a team plays as a whole determines its success. You may have the greatest bunch of individual stars in the world, but if they don't play together, the club won't be worth a dime." — Babe Ruth.

Several different areas must be considered when evaluating team dynamics of the job. How do the members of the executive team interact with each other? You may want to inquire about examples of how the team has managed challenges and adapted and how the team receives feedback.

What metrics and key performance indicators will you be judged on in your position? Do the individual team members' skills complement each other? How do they communicate with each other verbally and non-verbally? Does the team have "psychological safety" to provide feedback to the CEO and with each other when there is disagreement?

It is difficult to assess this in an interview, but asking explicitly and listening intently to the answers may provide some clues. Be sure to review the organizational chart and meet your direct reports if possible. The direct reports may be more open and transparent about the leadership dynamics.

It may be helpful to ask during the interview whether you can speak with some of the direct reports if it hasn't been offered, especially if you are heading into the final round. You may want to inquire about challenges related to team turnover, current challenges, accountability, communication style and organizational culture.

By asking strategic questions related to these aspects, you can gain a better understanding of the team's dynamics, performance, and potential fit within the organization.

REFERENCES

1. Seppälä E, Cameron K. Organizational Culture Proof That Positive Work Cultures Are More Productive. *Harvard Business Review* . December 1, 2015

2. Sawhney V. Career Planning Why Company Culture Matters: Our Favorite Reads. *Harvard Business Review*. December 3, 2021.

3. Church AH, Conger JA. Career Transitions When You Start a New Job, Pay Attention to These 5 Aspects of Company Culture. *Harvard Business Review*. March 29, 2018.

CHAPTER 8

How To Prepare Your Resume for a CMO Job

Gary A. Foster

REPARING A BRANDED CMO RESUME that is properly formatted, highly readable, and successful in conveying one's unique value proposition can be a daunting and time-consuming task, especially when attempted without guidance from a resume development specialist.

To begin with, remember that resumes, no matter how good they may be, don't get jobs. Resumes get conversations that lead to jobs.

Given that, and the fact that a resume is often a first impression, it is essential that an executive-level resume be crisp, clear, current, easy to read, and top-drawer in content, design, and flow.

The goal of this chapter is to provide the essential guidance for crafting a document that will accomplish this mission.

CURRICULUM VITAE (CV) OR RESUME?

What is most appropriate when looking for a CMO job: a CV or a resume?

I suggest a resume. Let's take a brief look at the difference to understand my reasoning.

Curriculum Vitae

A CV typically uses lists rather than a sentence/paragraph narrative presentation of content and individual accomplishments, usually leading off with education and dissertations followed by medical or academic posts, research, publications, presentations, awards, appointments, committees, and other professional engagements. CVs are generally more static and typically not tailored for specific jobs.

Thorough and often tedious, a CV can run into double-digit page length (I received one recently from a physician client that was 26 pages long) with much of the information extraneous to what a hiring authority for a CMO is looking for.

Resume

A resume is a marketing tool; it sells you to a potential employer. Briefer (usually 2–3 pages long), the resume includes information about your achievements, experience, education, and skills. When properly written, the resume tells a story that differentiates you and establishes your unique value proposition, profiles your skill set, and establishes how you have used that skill set to deliver results and benefits to your current and previous employers.

Another reason that a resume trumps a CV when pursuing a CMO position is that a typical CMO position includes activity-based requirements like those listed below that merit direct attention via the narrative format used in a resume.

- Clinical leadership
- Strategic planning
- Quality improvement
- Regulatory compliance
- Physician and staff relations
- Budget management
- Community and stakeholder engagement
- Research and innovation

Hybrid resume

Occasionally, it is appropriate to pull CV-like content into a resume, i.e., research studies, faculty positions, active committee involvement, and awards and honors. The decision on what is appropriate to add will be driven by the requirements of the position being considered.

CORE ELEMENTS OF A MODERN CMO RESUME

It's a tough job market, so you must do all you can to outshine your competition. The three resume components that will separate you from the pack are content, format, and design.

Content

Content is foremost in developing a resume. A poorly formatted and designed resume with great content will prevail over a smartly designed and formatted resume with poor or the wrong type of content.

As we think about content, it's helpful to remember the purpose of a resume. Your resume should:

1. Tell a story that differentiates you and establishes your unique value proposition.
2. Profile your skill set.
3. Establish how you have used both to deliver results and benefits to your current and previous employers.

With the development of content in mind, here are some tips and 15 questions to ask yourself to identify your unique value proposition (courtesy of my colleague and award-winning resume writer, Michelle Dumas):

Five tips:

1. **Self-assessment:** Find some time to seriously contemplate your career journey. Can you identify patterns? What specific challenges in your field have you consistently overcome? What specific strengths have you demonstrated and how have you leveraged those?
2. **Peer, supervisor, and mentor feedback:** Sometimes, others will see your value better than you do. Be bold. Ask those you work with and for about the unique value that they feel you deliver.
3. **Previous performance evaluations:** Hopefully, you've had performance evaluations across your career and kept them. Review them — they often highlight areas where you excel and unveil patterns of high performance.
4. **SWOT analysis:** Do a personal SWOT (strengths, weaknesses, opportunities, threats) analysis to help identify what you offer that others don't.
5. **Look for value beyond the job description:** What unofficial roles have you taken on in past positions that speak to your core strengths? Maybe it's particular committee work, mentoring roles, academic roles, community work, etc.

15 questions:

1. What problems am I particularly good at solving?

2. In what ways do I have the ability to make my employers money or save them money?
3. Do I stand out in my ability to increase efficiency or productivity?
4. What value can I bring to the company that other candidates cannot?
5. What is the "legacy" of value I have left at past employing companies?
6. What are my top three professional achievements, and what skills or qualities did I use to achieve them?
7. Have I ever improved a process, system, or approach at work? What was the impact?
8. What tasks or projects energize me the most, and why?
9. How have I adapted to changes or challenges in my previous roles, and what did I learn from those experiences?
10. What feedback do I consistently receive from peers, supervisors, or subordinates about my work or approach?
11. In what areas do I consistently outperform my peers or exceed expectations?
12. What unique perspectives or experiences do I bring to my profession or industry?
13. How do I handle setbacks or failures, and what do they teach me?
14. What additional responsibilities have I taken on outside of my official job description, and why?
15. If I were to ask my colleagues to describe me in three words, what would they say?

A serious commitment to using these tips and writing out answers to these questions will serve you well in developing a resume that will help ensure that you make the cut for consideration for the job you have in your headlights.

Format and Design

With the content collected and organized, plugging it into a professional, executive-level format and design is the next step. Let's look at the format first.

The format that I generally use for a physician executive resume includes these components:

- Name and contact details

- Title of Current Position or the Position Being Sought
- Branding Statement
- Executive Summary
- Skills and Qualifications/Core Competencies
- Achievement Highlights
- Professionals Experience
- Education
- Certifications & Affiliations
- Board Memberships
- Community/Volunteer Activities
- Optional: Academic Experience; Awards & Honors; Military Experience; Key Publications

I'll draw from a collection of physician executive resumes that I've done (altered to protect privacy) to illustrate the various components.

Name and Contact Details

Your name should be prominent and in the largest font size on the document. I compose mostly in sans serif Calibri or Arial fonts and usually start with the name in 20 pt font. Along with the name, it is important to include the acronyms for education and appropriate certifications.

Contact details should be phone, city, state, and zip code (no street address), email, and customized LinkedIn URL.

Eric Schwartz
MD, MBA , FACP

832.123.4567 ❖ Suburbia, TX 77401 ❖ eric.schwartz@email.com ❖ linkedin.com/in/eric.t.schwartz

Title, Branding Statement, and Executive Summary

This illustrates the title, a self-developed branding statement, and an executive summary.

The title clarifies your job target and is a statement of intent. Recruiters/ hiring managers look first for the title on a resume to make sure that it aligns with what they are looking for. Thus, the title must also be prominent and in large, bolded font (18 pt font, in this case).

Chief Medical Officer

Leading patient-centric, value-based care delivery at the appropriate site of service.
Physician executive with extensive value-based care background and hands-on clinical experience. Respected thought leader and innovator of processes, particularly in development of service lines that make healthcare more accessible and affordable. Collaborative and effective communicator who combines business acumen, strategic planning ability, and subject-matter-expert understanding of value-based care delivery to develop programs that fill care-need gaps in the community while producing savings for the health plan. Builds solid relationships with hospital/provider partners leading to improved care coordination through better communication between inpatient and outpatient care providers.

Skills and Qualifications

Sometimes titled "Core Competencies" or "Signature Strengths," this section assembles and draws attention to the competencies you've acquired and demonstrated across your career. It also displays important keywords and keyword phrases that may be found in the job description and picked up by an applicant tracking system.

> Health System Strategy | Hospital Clinical Operations | Medical Group Management | Value-Based Care
> Payor Relationships | Financial Management & Stewardship | Physician Alignment & Productivity
> Quality & Patient Safety Transformation | Telehealth | Clinical Research | GME | CMS Advisory

This top portion of the resume is critical. It tells much of your story and injects critical keywords and keyword phrases that an application tracking system may be looking for.

Achievement Highlights

Consider including a section that profiles a handful of high-impact achievements to draw more — and early — attention to how your skills have been deployed to produce top-tier results. These generally will be stated in a brief and broader overview style as they may be amplified further in the resume.

Career Highlights

❖ **Strategically planned and executed programs** that reduced inpatient costs and created significant financial savings for the health plan while simultaneously creating a coordinated continuum for value-based healthcare delivery across a metro area with 7M+ population.

❖ **Expanded hospitalist coverage fourfold** in the Greater Xxxxxx market.

❖ **Created strong reciprocal relationships with 20+ hospital partners through excellent people skills,** leading to improved care coordination through better inpatient and outpatient provider communications.

❖ **Established and led several new in-clinic employed-physician service lines** that expanded market reach and addressed critical gaps in specialty healthcare coverage in the Greater Xxxxxx Area.

❖ **Selected by State Medical Association as a founding member of the Committee on Alternate Payment Methods** to address the knowledge gap amongst the physician community regarding nuances of Value-based Care plans.

Professional Experience

The work experience section of the resume is often the most underdeveloped area yet one of the most important.

The three most common shortfalls in executive healthcare resumes are:

1. Failure to describe the scope and size of the current and previous employers. Recruiters or hiring managers typically are seeking someone who has experience within an organization of similar or larger size and scope and need to know how your work experience compares.
2. Limited description of the scope of the main responsibilities of the position.
3. Substituting responsibilities for achievements and failure to provide quality, results-based, quantifiable accomplishments.

To address these shortfalls, using a three-part format as illustrated below works best where the facility and location are clearly identified, followed by a description of the size and scope of the facility.

The title of the position is then followed by a description of the major responsibilities along with some details about the scope of the job, such as number of direct reports, total FTEs, budget managed, number of facilities, etc.

The most critical part of the Experience section is high-impact and quantifiable achievements. This is the biggest challenge because there is a tendency to confuse responsibilities and achievements; not every achievement is quantifiable or metric-based. I guide clients by helping them understand the different levels of achievement.

Achievements should be diverse, covering multiple categories: leadership, financial, operational, human resources, board, etc.

Achievements come in three tiers:

Tier One – This is the most powerful and should always include quantifiable metrics, such as revenue enhancement, cost reduction, time savings, turnover reduction, etc., with an absolute number or percentage. Examples of Tier One achievements are:

- Accelerated cash by $750K with an 80% reduction in receivables beyond 90 days.
- Led recruitment and employment strategy to support hiring more than 2,600 associates per year on a budget of $2.1M, equating to an

average cost per hire of $890 (over three years), compared to an average external vendor fee of $5,000 per hire.

Tier Two – A good example would be a success-based on a limited time frame. For example: You developed and implemented a project, but left before it launched. Your success would be based on the time you were involved and not necessarily on metrics that we would see in a Tier One achievement. In this example, two successes could be: (1) consultants and a new team were brought into the development of the project, and (2) you have calculated a quick breakeven point and projected a profit in the first year. Examples of Tier Two achievements are:

- Appointed interim CMO at XYZ Hospital for 90 days. Hired an OB/GYN within first 30 days and helped save hospital from immediate closure.
- Accelerated safety culture with educational initiative of high-reliability organization for 1,000 employees by creating a new onboarding program.

Tier Three – The weakest of all tiers, but when all else fails, use an action word to imply success (energized, rejuvenated, enhanced, successful, etc.). If they cannot fit into these Top Three Tiers, they do not belong. Examples of Tier Three achievements are:

- Enhanced revenue cycle team competencies by starting a financial leadership mentor program.
- Launched pediatric open-heart program through a 10-year partnership with XYZ Hospital.

How many achievements?

Don't try to unpack your entire work history in this document. Resist the temptation to tell it all and turn an Experience section into what I refer to as a "polka-dotted obituary" with too much information and far too many bullet points. I recommend restricting the list of high-impact achievements (Tier One, preferably) to 5-8 across each of your last two experiences and fewer the further back you go.

How far back should you go?

In the reverse chronology format I am illustrating, you don't need to provide much, if any, detail for positions older than 10 years. At most, 15 years, but only if in that extra five years there is something that speaks loudly to your career progression or to an activity that was a major contributor to your current success.

I typically don't ignore or eliminate experiences older than 10–15 years but rather include a mention of them in a separate section entitled "Additional Relevant Experience" or "Early Career." It may be important to include them to illustrate the progressive nature of your career path and the early activities that helped chart the path for your current career success.

Professional Experience

Anywhere Regional Medical Center (ARMC), Anywhere, USA   7/2011 to Present
Community acute care hospital with 406 beds, 3,000 employees, and 525 medical staff offering comprehensive, state-of-the-art medical care and services to the residents of Anywhere and the surrounding communities. Services include a Cancer Center, Psychiatry, Electrophysiology, Endocrinology, Plastic Surgery, Colorectal Surgery, Robotic Surgery, Orthopedic Surgery, and Sports Medicine.

CHIEF MEDICAL OFFICER & VICE PRESIDENT OF MEDICAL AFFAIRS (10/2015 to Present)
Supervise 250+ employed medical staff including physicians and APPs, medical staff office, quality and provider support department, Graduate Medical Education (GME) program, Regional Health Collaborative Clinically Integrated Network (CIN), and transitional care services.
Notable Achievements:
- ❖ Added 16 new service lines to the community, radically improved primary care physician coverage through aggressive recruitment and addition of 2 primary care clinics, and grew provider group from 22 to 285 in 5 years.
- ❖ Improved average first-available new primary care patient appointment from 42-60 days to 5 days.
- ❖ Succeeded in gaining approval through state legislature for $1.5M in funding and expansion of family medicine and primary care residency from 18 to 24 over 3 years with 60% of residents remaining in the community.
- ❖ Launched larger value-based strategy combining 6 value-based agreements, simplifying point-of-care, and covering 25,000 lives (10% of the county population).
- ❖ Reduced hospital readmission rates by 1/3 (18% to 12%) by bringing local sub-acute programs (nursing homes, acute rehab, hospice, home health) into a common framework using quarterly meetings to share best practices.
- ❖ Created wellness committee for medical staff and Chief Wellness Office with part-time organizational psychologist to address performance and communication issues, burnout, and declining patient experience scores. Success rate at 70%.
- ❖ Saved $3.6M and reduced excess hospital length-of-stay (LOS) from 5,000 to 3,500 hours in 2021 by establishing new guidelines for hospitalists and a Rapid Decision Unit.

The balance of the resume can be finished out with the following sections:

Early Career

Schwartz Oncology, Upstate, NY,   2004 to 2015

GYNECOLOGIC ONCOLOGIST
Managed all aspects of solo practice, providing diagnosis and surgical management of cancerous and noncancerous conditions of the female reproductive system.

Bayfield Obstetrics and Gynecology, Upstate, NY   2003 to 2004
Medical group practice specializing in Obstetrics & Gynecology.

GYNECOLOGIC ONCOLOGIST

Education

Master in Healthcare Management, Harvard T.H. Chan School of Public Health, Cambridge, MA	2020
Fellowship in Gynecologic Oncology, Cleveland Clinic Foundation, Cleveland, OH	2002
Residency in Obstetrics and Gynecology, Albert Einstein College of Medicine, Bronx, NY	1999
Doctor of Medicine, George Washington University School of Medicine and Health Sciences, Washington, DC	1995
Bachelor of Arts, Political Science, and Government, Dartmouth College, Hanover, NH	1991

Certifications & Licensure

Gynecologic Oncology, Board Certified	2011
Obstetrics and Gynecology, Board Certified	2004
State of New York License #1234567	

Professional Affiliations

New York Obstetrical Society, Member

Society of Gynecologic Oncology, Member & Finance Committee, Member

Fellow American College of Surgeons (FACS)

Fellow American College of Obstetricians and Gynecologists (FACOG)

Society of Laparoendoscopic Surgeons, Member

American Association of Gynecologic Laparoscopists, Member

American Association of Cancer Research, Member

American Society of Clinical Oncology, Member

American Medical Association, Member

Honors & Awards

C-SATS Expert in Gynecologic Oncology, Online Reviewer of Robotic Surgery for Quality Review	2017 to 2022
Master Surgeon in Robotic Surgery, Surgical Review Corporation	2019 to 2022
Master Surgeon in Minimally Invasive Gynecology, Surgical Review Corporation	2019 to 2022
Board Examiner, American Board of OB/GYN	2019 to 2022

Committees

ABCD Health Physician Partners Executive Committee	2020 to 2022
ABCD Health Physician Partners Board of Governors	2020 to 2022
System Ambulatory Operations Committee	2020 to 2022
System Peri-op Value Committee, Chairman	2020 to 2022
Upstate Univ Hospital Physician Leadership Committee	2016 to 2022
OB/GYN Service Line Performance Improvement Committee	2015 to 2022

Examples of additional sections to consider:

Faculty Positions

Associate Professor, Department of Emergency Medicine, Univ. of Anywhere, Downtown, WA	**2021 to Present**
Assistant Professor, Department of Emergency Medicine, Univ. of Anywhere, Downtown, WA	**2017 to 2021**
Clinical Instructor, Department of Emergency Medicine, Ivy Univ. School of Medicine, Boston, MA	**2013 to 2015**

Military Service

Major, U.S. Air Force Medical Corps, XXst Medical Group, Staff Cardiologist and Director, Cardiac Cath Lab
Developed the first coronary artery stent program and Acute MI intervention program for Department of Defense Region X, Supervised 6 cardiologists. Received "Meritorious Service Medal" in 1997.

Preferably as it would apply to your professional experience/career development

Community/Volunteer Activities

Citywide Academy of Medicine, President, 2003 to 2004
Medical Society of (State) Foundation, President, 2008 to 2009
Citizens Academy, Suburbia, VA 2006
Citywide Beacon of Hope, President, 2013 to 2015; Board Member, 2012 to 2018

Ideally, these would be activities that link to your professional position.

Design

A few words on the design. Basic, bland, black-and-white text resumes written in Times New Roman font are old school. No, your resume doesn't need to be overly fancy or heavily designed. In fact, because of my executive healthcare background and the feedback I get from the executive healthcare recruiting community, I rarely design resumes with graphics, charts, or graphs, for two reasons: (1) they don't get read by applicant tracking systems and (2) experienced recruiters consider them to be unnecessary clutter.

The resume should be designed first and foremost to be strategic with appropriate flow but with some design distinction to make it more interesting, to aid the reader, and give the résumé visual appeal that makes it stand apart from the typical self-developed resume. I favor using colors in the section headings as illustrated earlier.

In a resume, less can be more.

SUMMARY

- Tell the story of "you" as a problem-solver, solutions-provider, and people-builder.
- Maximize metrics and "wow" with results centered on the problems the prospective position needs solved.
- Read your resume with your hiring hat on and ask yourself these questions:
  - "Would I want to pick up the phone and call this person?"
  - "Would this person make my life easier?"
  - "Based on what I see, would I feel confident that I could work with this person?"

CHAPTER 9

How to Interview for a Chief Medical Officer Job

Mark D. Olszyk, MD, MBA, CPE, FACEP, FACHE, FAAPL, FFSMB

A S A PHYSICIAN, IT IS not a stretch to say that every patient encounter is an interview. Yet, it is much different when you are the one being asked the questions.

Like many of you, my first real interviews began with the process of college and medical school applications. Then residency. And then for various jobs and positions. I have been interviewed by government officials, military officers, private sector executives, as well as peers and folks who will report to me.

In some of the interviews I got an instant good vibe. When that happened, the interview was easy and a lot of fun. In others, I had a bad feeling from the first minute. Then, the interview became a self-fulfilling prophecy and every effort to get back on track seemed to backfire. After every interview, I walk away wondering how it went so right so easily or got off track so quickly.

There is always an unknown element when people come together with all their expectations and experiences. Like a chess game, after a few minutes there are innumerable possible directions the interview can take. Even after having done this for a while, I am still learning how best to interview and be interviewed.

Over the past 25 years in medical leadership, I have conducted more than 1,000 interviews. For some interviews, I was the final decision maker; for others, I was one of the chief decision makers. For a few, I was the sole decision maker; for others I was part of a large panel with only minimal influence.

I have interviewed candidates to work with me, to be my colleague or peer, to be my boss, or to work in a different hospital or different part of the organization. I have also interviewed or screened candidates to be contributors on a project or to a book or to work on committees completely outside of healthcare.

As a scoutmaster, I held dozens of meetings with young men to assess their understanding of their rank advancements, achievements, and implementing the Scout Code into their lives.

We like to think that an interview will yield some clarity in the selection process once the field is narrowed down to a few candidates. However, given the limited amount of time in a somewhat artificial set-up, the interview is in essence a process to discern the mind of another. Learning about and appreciating someone's personality, drives, and reactions is something that can take a lifetime — certainly not an hour.

The interview is a snapshot impression that a hiring decision is predicated on. Even when we increase the scrutiny — such as for credentialing and privileging physicians, adding background checks and letters of recommendation — we still occasionally hire someone who is not a good fit.

I recall a few instances when the candidate I was interviewing registered a favorable impression in the first few seconds. Malcolm Gladwell talks about that in his book *Blink*.[1] Yet, even though I got a good vibe and thought we had an excellent interview, the candidate turned out to be a less than ideal choice. That begs the question: What is the value of an interview, if any?

Some experts say it is a valuable and essential part of the process. Others say it is far too subjective to have any real value. Proponents see interviewing as a way for the employer to determine if the applicant's skills, background, and personality meet their requirements. It also helps the employer determine if an applicant will fit in with the culture. The process itself helps focus the candidate and ensure that they understand the expectations of the employer.[2]

An interview is a critical aspect of the hiring process. Combined with a good impression and solid resume, a good interview can be the deciding factor and lead to a job offer.[3]

TYPES OF INTERVIEWS

There are several types of interviews:

Structured Interview. The interviewer(s) have a checklist of topics and questions to ask each candidate as a means to inform the hiring decision. This checklist can be crucial to guard against allegations of discrimination, as all applicants are asked the same questions. This also should reduce inter-rater variability.

Unstructured Interview. There is no checklist of standard questions; rather, the applicant and the interviewer(s) hold a free-flowing conversation. Questions are open-ended. A benefit of this strategy is that the candidates may disclose more information about themselves than they would have by answering close-ended questions. Also, the interviewer can ask nuanced or detailed follow-up questions based on the candidates' answers. However, the lack of structure makes it difficult to compare and rank applicants. Some examples of open-ended questions are:

- Describe a situation in which you were able to use persuasion to successfully convince someone to see things your way.
- Describe a time when you were faced with a stressful situation that you demonstrated your coping skills.
- Give me a specific example of a time when you used good judgment and logic in solving a problem.[4]

You can find lists of open-ended, performance-based questions online.

Situational Interview. In this format, the candidate is given a problem or fictional scenario to respond to, such as: *You have been hired as the director in a 500-person company. You are struggling to meet certain performance metrics. Your boss tells you that you need to be more strategic. How would you handle this situation? What are your priorities? What framework would you use to assess, act, follow up, and analyze the results?*

Situational interviews can be elevated by simulation. For example, to assess my skills of negotiation and personality management, I was cast as the chief operating officer at a C-suite meeting. One of the team members played an angry physician, another played an aggrieved party, and the others were executives with certain agendas. I believe this was a much more realistic test of my skills than having me answer a theoretical question in an office.

Group Interview. This strategy involves panels of interviewers — ideally no more than four or five. One of the group interviews in which I was the candidate took place in a large boardroom with about 15 people of various titles and backgrounds. It was a friendly group and the format was a free-flowing discussion, which I enjoyed.

Another was conducted over Zoom during the pandemic. It was hard to focus on anybody in particular and I certainly could not read their body language. In addition, some of them were distracted; a few clearly were looking at their cell phones or elsewhere. This format was not very conducive for an interview.

One-way Interview. Ostensibly to be more efficient and flexible and have the opportunity to evaluate more candidates, some interviews are conducted one-way. It is akin to a screen test for an actor or a demo tape for a vocal artist. The candidate receives a link and is given a certain amount of time to answer each question that appears once the link is activated. The candidate is videotaped while responding spontaneously to each question.

This format puts a lot of pressure on the candidate. There is no way to read the audience and adjust an answer; however, it certainly is efficient for the interviewers. They can watch the performance asynchronously whenever they like — whether as a panel or individually.

To prepare for a one-way interview, I recommend you practice answering likely questions and record yourself several times before doing it for real.

PREPARING FOR THE INTERVIEW

When preparing for the interview, consider the interviewer's task. They need to rank you among several other candidates. They will look at your most important qualities, experiences, and education, as well as the characteristics that they think a successful candidate possesses.

Prior to the interview, make a list of all the qualities, skills, and experiences that you want to highlight during your interview. Also, be prepared to answer these common questions:

- What are you looking to gain from your next position?
- Why do you want to work for our company?
- Why did you leave your last job?
- Tell me about your relationship with your previous manager: How was it productive? How could it have been improved?

Make the first 60 seconds matter. Prepare yourself mentally. Try to relax as much as possible so you can appear calm and collected. Dress professionally and in keeping with the culture of the hiring entity. Arrive early, whether it's a Zoom interview or in person, but realize that your early arrival may prompt the interview to begin early, robbing you of some time to compose yourself beforehand.

If the interview is in-person, walk into the room like you own it. Pause, look around, adopt an expansive posture. Always pay attention to your body language. Sit up straight, use appropriate gestures, be confident, and make eye contact. Smile. Speak deliberately and precisely. Pay attention to the interviewer's body language.

At the beginning of the interview, ask how many minutes you have and if there are a set number of questions. State that you want to be respectful of everyone's time and consider everyone's questions. If you have an hour for an interview and there are 15 questions, ask if you can pace yourself accordingly. That will show foresight and respect. It will also put you more in charge of the interview. Follow up your responses by asking: *Does that answer your question? Is that the kind of information you are looking for?*

I once had a 45-minute interview and answered each question in detail as it was asked of me. Afterwards, I found out that because of time constraints, not everyone had the chance to ask their questions. I wish they had been upfront with the format, but as the candidate, it was my responsibility to understand the playing field. Ask for the rules upfront, in a friendly manner.

By all means avoid sarcasm or obscure humor. Also, do not be afraid of silences. Candidates often feel compelled to fill up all the possible time and that can lead to rapid speech or inartful phrases. While a comfortable speech rate is about 120 words a minute, we can think about 10 times faster. That mismatch can negatively affect the answers we give as we try to pour too much thought into too little time.

Extroverts do better in interviews because they are more comfortable in social situations. For the purposes of the interview, dial up the extroversion. Make small talk when appropriate, sell yourself, engage with the interviewer, and be succinct and direct.

INTERVIEW PITFALLS

Although the interview, however limited, is of some use, it can be a poor predictor of performance. An interview reveals only a sample of someone's behavior and personality — and an unrealistic one at that. Would you get married after a first date?

Yet, interviews are a standard part of the hiring process. Realizing that the interview is inevitable, what lessons can be drawn from this counterpoint to enhance your interview performance?

Interviews lack what psychologists call ecological validity.[5] The candidate's behavior in an interview does not necessarily reflect the behavior they will exhibit or need in the job itself.

We tend to look at and interpret information to confirm our biases. If our first impression of a candidate is favorable, we are more likely to approve of their answers to questions. This is called the halo effect. (The opposite effect, the horn effect, can also occur).

We also tend to be biased toward physically attractive people, toward people who remind us of someone we like, or toward someone who resembles us in some way or with whom we have something in common, such as a favorite sports team.

Preparation is critical to an interview, but it does have its pitfalls. In one of my more successful interviews, I did a lot of pre-interview research. I knew the biographies of all my interviewers. I knew the statistics and metrics publicly available about the hospital. I even toured the hospital as a "secret shopper." I did a lot of homework and it showed.

For another interview, my homework backfired. I did my research and had answers for everything I thought they would ask. One of the interviewers was a medical oncologist so I wrote down the three most commonly prescribed oncology meds. I thought they would ask me about being a scoutmaster, so I also wrote out the scout oath. I had so much material and data in front of me and I didn't want to waste all that effort I had put into my preparation, so I just kept spouting facts instead of relaxing.

I am sure I seemed a bit rushed and maybe even pedantic. The authentic me did not come across. Sure enough, the evaluation from the hiring firm was that I did not come across as genuine. That was strange for me to hear because that has consistently been one of my most commented-on traits. You *can* sabotage yourself.

DO YOUR RESEARCH

It is good to know what the real chances are of you getting the job. Ask the recruiter or screener or HR rep how many candidates there are and if there are any internal candidates. I once had a very successful interview and I thought I was a shoo-in, but the process was a mere formality; they already had an inside candidate marked for selection. If I had known that from the outset, of course I wouldn't have put myself through the process.

It's good to be able to show the interviewers that you have done your homework and made the effort to learn about the organization. If you have colleagues or friends within the organization you're interviewing for, reach out to them for background information (nothing confidential). Check the organizations' social media profiles. Do extensive research on the job description and the company. Look at similar job descriptions in other companies. This research at the very least will indicate to the interviewer that you have interest in the field. When you share a story make sure it has a purpose and is succinct with a beginning, a middle, and an end. You do not need to reiterate anything on your application or your resume.

Always keep your stories positive. Never throw anybody under the bus. Organizations want to hire someone who will fit in and contribute to workplace harmony. You are not going to make a favorable impression by saying that your former or about to be former colleagues were suboptimal or non-supportive or malicious. Just say you had an amazing team and you loved coming to work. Never single out anybody or talk negatively about anybody. Elevate others and always appear to be a team player.

At the end of the interview, they will ask if you have any questions. Be prepared with a few. For example: *Can you tell me about the expected workload for fulfilling administrative duties versus clinical duties? How much day-to-day medical practice am I expected to do? Is there anything about my experience that might make you hesitant about my ability to fulfill the expectations of this leadership position?*

Even if you don't get the job, don't feel too bad. On average, every corporate job gets about 250 resumes. Of those, a handful will get called for an interview and, of course, only one person will get the job.

REFERENCES

1. Gladwell M. *Blink: The Power of Thinking without Thinking.* New York: Little, Brown and Co., 2005.
2. SHRM. Interviewing Candidates for Employment. Toolkit. https://www.shrm.org/resourcesandtools/tools-and-samples/toolkits/pages/interviewingcandidatesforemployment.aspx

3. TeamStage. Job Interview Statistics: Applications and Hiring Rates in 2024. blog. https://teamstage.io/job-interview-statistics/

4. Diaz NM. Interview Question: Persuasion & Convincing Someone to See Your Way. My Perfect Resume blog. December 5, 2022. https://www.myperfectresume.com/career-center/interviews/questions/describe-a-situation-where-you-had-to-establish-your-point-of-view

5. Shpancer N. Poor Predictors: Job Interviews Are Useless and Unfair. Psychology Today blog. August 31, 2020. www.psychologytoday.com/us/blog/insight-therapy/202008/poor-predictors-job-interviews-are-useless-and-unfair.

Advice from Those Who Have Held These Roles

CHAPTER 10

The Hospital CMO

Reka Danko, MD

THE ANNOUNCEMENT "CODE BLUE, ROOM 722," reverberates through the hospital. Someone is experiencing a cardiopulmonary arrest.

Team members from various hospital locations swiftly converge on the announced room. One starts CPR, another retrieves and opens the crash cart, and someone prepares medications while confirming or establishing intravenous access. Simultaneously, one team member pulls up medical records, and another records intervention timings, adhering to the evidence-based protocol. Family members and friends are escorted out and comforted, or efforts are made to locate loved ones to keep them informed.

Regardless of how many code blue events one attends, they are always intense — someone's life is at stake, and everyone is doing their utmost to help the patient in need. Code Blue events also highlight the remarkable teamwork in hospitals, where people come together instantly to help someone in a dire situation — people saving people.

The hospital chief medical officer (CMO) has the opportunity to establish the highest quality medical programs and enlighten non-clinical executives about the best practices in medicine and their secure implementation.

OVERVIEW OF HOSPITAL OPERATIONS

According to the American Hospital Association's Fast Facts, there were a total of 6,129 hospitals in the United States in 2023, with 919,649 licensed hospital beds. Regardless of their differences, all these hospitals share a common characteristic: They function as homes for the sickest individuals, those too unwell to thrive at home or in other care facilities.

The most critically ill patients require the most intensive care, demanding around-the-clock assessments and interventions. This involves a multitude of individuals with various expertise: preparing medications, conducting lab analyses, performing tests, administering medications, monitoring vital signs or assessment changes, creating special diets, and maintaining clean rooms and equipment, along with well-stocked supplies.

Unlike most homes and businesses, hospitals operate continuously throughout the day and night, all year long. Operating 24/7 requires substantial labor resources and supplies. Due to their intensity, hospitals are also the most expensive to operate. To keep hospitals open, cost-effective strategies must be identified, similar to any other business.

The only constant in medicine is continual change. Medical advancements have expanded treatment options, introduced new medications, facilitated less invasive testing and interventions, and improved the safety and efficacy of surgeries. Medicine is progressively shifting toward outpatient settings with the advent of ambulatory surgery centers, hospital in-home programs, and infusion programs.

Patients now have more opportunities for treatment outside the hospital. Recognizing the inherent risks in hospitals, it becomes crucial to limit the time patients spend in these settings. Since hospitals represent the most intensive and expensive level of care, coupled with associated risks, it is imperative to strengthen the continuity of care from pre-hospitalization to post-hospitalization.

When hospitalization is unavoidable, the goal is to minimize the patient's time in the hospital. Understanding the available resources and care options outside the hospital in your community is essential. Collaborating with these resources and various care levels helps optimize efficiency for hospitals and other care centers.

In explaining the physiological experience during hospitalization, I draw a parallel between the human body and a car ascending a hill. When the body is in good health, it requires minimal necessities such as food, water, safety, and sleep. However, during hospitalization, at least one acute process is at play, be it an infection, organ dysfunction, body trauma, or an exacerbation of one or multiple conditions. This places the body in a state of stress, rapidly depleting energy from within.

The heightened stress cycles and hormones exert additional pressure on the system, demanding more energy. The immune system becomes strained, and weakness sets in rapidly. Sometimes, even a single day in the hospital may necessitate over a week of rehabilitation to return to the prior baseline status, even without complications.

During periods of stress and illness, appetite is often reduced, and coupled with hospital food rather than one's favorite meals, oral intake can be severely diminished. Poor sleep patterns due to being outside their own beds and subjected to a schedule of assessments and interventions further complicate the patient's recovery process. Healing is more effective when social and environmental supports boost emotional health. However, hospitals are often places of uncertainty, fear, and vulnerability, intensifying patient stress and impeding the healing process.

Staying in a hospital can lead to well-known complications, including those arising from inserted catheters, lines, and tubes, decreased activity levels, impacts on thinking and cognition, disruptions to normal digestion, and exposure to serious infections prevalent in hospitals.

Given these factors, it is optimal to discharge patients from the hospital as soon as possible. This clinical concept should be conveyed to all team members. Nurses can assist with early mobility protocols, aiming to make patients as functional as possible as early as possible in their hospital stay.

Physical and occupational therapies play a vital role in implementing mobility protocols and encouraging patients to return to the safest and lowest level of care promptly. Despite being exhausted and in pain, patients should be informed that any level of movement aids blood flow, natural healing, and prevents muscle wasting and further complications.

QUALITY METRICS

Every member of the hospital staff influences hospital length of stay. Maximizing all workflows, including timely tests, having medications and supplies ready, efficient bed turnovers, and ensuring that patients requiring fasting before tests or procedures do not receive meal trays, all contribute to the patient's journey.

Quality metrics play a crucial role in guiding high-quality care and ensuring specific benchmarks are met for certain diseases. Understanding the basis of these metrics and initiatives is essential for effective collaboration when everyone comprehends the shared goals and rationale.

Clinical teams should grasp the importance of providing quality care along with accurate and effective documentation. Documentation serves as the narrative of the patient's illness, describing the what and why of interventions in the hospital. Patients should receive the highest quality care at the right level for healthcare delivery to function optimally.

Optimizing prevention and chronic disease management through outpatient primary and specialty care is vital. Patients should have access to providers and care managers for assistance with acute medical problems and addressing the social determinants of health.

When outpatient management is exhausted, and patients need a more intensive level of care, hospitals step in to continue that medically necessary care. Medical necessity has evolved over time, shaping the landscape of healthcare delivery.

COSTS OF CARE AND CASE MANAGEMENT

Not all care within the hospital is inpatient care. Medical necessity is a prerequisite for inpatient hospital care, and outpatient levels of hospital care also exist — observation care and bedded outpatient (also known as extended outpatient services or outpatient in a bed [OPIB]). Since we observe patients in hospitals and monitor their clinical responses, many may not think of observation care as an outpatient level of care covered under Medicare Part B (outpatient services) rather than Medicare Part A, which covers inpatient hospital services.

Observation status entails using a hospital bed for monitoring or patient care necessary to evaluate an outpatient condition while determining the need for an inpatient admission. Observation indicates lower severity of illness and resource intensity. If the patient's illness severity increases or additional treatment escalation is required, consideration should be given to inpatient admission.

Observation hospitalizations have increased over time as national criteria have tightened inpatient medical necessity criteria, and some diagnoses transition to inpatient admission only for life-threatening conditions or after "failing observation" care. Observation care is not dictated by a time frame but instead by medical necessity criteria.

Although many healthcare payers designate a maximum number of hours in observation care, it does not guarantee that medical necessity criteria will be met at the completion of the maximum observation hours. Conditions must require ongoing or escalating treatments and evaluations for inpatient medical necessity.

Previously, hospitals were paid based on the actual cost of care. When this cost became burdensome, an awareness developed regarding which conditions and which patients required care in the hospital. The Diagnosis Related Group (DRG) system was developed to monitor the costs of care and the utilization of services in hospitals.

The DRG classification system is based on diagnoses to relate the types of patients being treated to the overall costs of care. DRG classifies the patient's case by principal diagnosis and other comorbid (CC) or major comorbid (MCC) conditions or complications. The lists of DRGs, as well as the CCs and MCCs, are published and updated yearly. It is important to familiarize oneself with the DRG system and with the CCs and MCCs, as these are the complications and comorbid conditions that increase the severity of illness.

The collective complexity of cases in the hospital is determined from the DRGs and called the case mix index, which is the marker of how sick the patients are who require care in the hospital. DRG also determines the geometric mean length of stay (GMLOS), which is defined as the number of days given to each patient based on the principal diagnosis, secondary conditions, and surgery if applicable. Since GMLOS is calculated based on diagnoses, it reflects the average time that patients with similar conditions should stay in the hospital.

GMLOS is a guide to help with length of stay management. Since GMLOS also guides the cost of care allotted to the patient with those specific conditions, hospitals perform best financially when the average hospital length of stay is at or under the average GMLOS. Hospital-acquired complications are exempt from a higher DRG category to prevent potential rewards for compromising quality of care.

Another way to understand case mix complexity is to break down its components. Once we understand the key terms of severity of illness, prognosis, treatment difficulty, need for intervention, and resource intensity, we may begin to teach these concepts to others.

First, let's remind ourselves that hospitals are homes for the sick and deliver one part in the continuum of care. The hospital portion of care is meant to be short-term and high acuity, so this is important to both understand and to document well. Severity of illness relates to the loss of function and risk of mortality that a patient experiences from a certain illness or illnesses. Prognosis is the predicted outcome related to the illness, possible deterioration, or recurrence of the illnesses and, in some cases, may include predictions about the life span. Treatment difficulty refers to the management of the patient's care due to specific illnesses—such as complex required procedures or close monitoring and assessments.

The need for intervention describes what consequences would happen if the care were not immediately performed or continued. Resource intensity describes the volume and types of diagnostic and therapeutic services required for the management of certain illnesses. In the simplest breakdown, patients in the hospital must (1) be sick and must (2) require hospital-level resources and interventions. If patients are being monitored without interventions or if the interventions are all available in a lower level of care, does the patient really require hospital-level care?

THE IMPORTANCE OF DOCUMENTATION

Telling the story specific to the patient, their illnesses, and the need to be in the hospital is important for transmitting accurate documentation to support medical necessity, quality of care, rationale for care, and recording the details of the hospital portion of the care continuum for the patient and their clinical teams.

Per the Centers for Medicare and Medicaid Services (CMS), the two-midnight standard rule is a policy that applies to inpatient hospital admissions where the patient is reasonably expected to stay at least two midnights, and this expectation is documented in the medical record by the clinician.

Medical evidence should be documented, such as the risk of an adverse event during hospitalization and the complexity of the patient's conditions and what assessments and treatment will be needed for the acute illness(es). Considerations in documentation would include the medical history and comorbid conditions, severity of the presenting complaints, medical needs of the patient, and the risk of adverse events and mortality.

The two-midnight expectation and the daily hospital progress and care provided are crucial to telling the story of the hospitalization. At times, the patient's length of stay may not span the expected two midnights. In these situations, it is important to complete accurate documentation explaining why the length of stay did not meet the initial clinical expectation. Examples of such unforeseen circumstances would be a patient leaving against medical advice, the election of hospice services, a recovery that was faster than expected, transfer for a higher level of care, or death.

Additionally, CMS publishes the inpatient-only list yearly, which is a list of the surgeries that are required to be done in a hospital inpatient setting due to the complexity of the surgeries or postoperative care required. The surgeries found on the inpatient-only list do not require a two-midnight stay expectation. According to the CMS final rule 2023, Medicare Advantage plans will also be required to use the two-midnight rule beginning in 2024.

Health plans, including Medicare Advantage, commercial, and Managed Medicaid plans, have the opportunity to use other criteria for medical necessity. Different plans use various criteria; some even use more than one set or self-written criteria layered on top of nationally published criteria. The most utilized of these criteria are the MCG Guidelines and InterQual. Both of these criteria require subscriptions for access and are ever-changing. The Milliman Care Guidelines (MCG) were developed in 1988 by a global actuarial and consulting firm, Milliman, and collaborating physicians to form the first evidence-based care guidelines based on risk-versus-benefit calculations. MCG was acquired by Hearst Corporation, a large, diversified media and information company, in 2012. (See www.mcg.com for details.)

InterQual was developed in 1976 and is owned by Change Healthcare, which was acquired in 2021 by Optum, a healthcare analytics company owned by UnitedHealth Group. (See www.changehealthcare.com for details.) Federal lawsuits by the Department of Justice attempted unsuccessfully to halt the acquisition of the InterQual decision support tool by a health insurance company due to the potential for conflicts of interest.

The most effective strategy to help hospitals is to get to know the breakdown of payers at the hospital and understand which criteria they use. Discuss the contracts and how they work. Understand if the contracts are fee-for-service or based on DRGs; this will help in the prevention and management of denied claims. Building a connection to the payers is a necessary strategy to work together to help your mutual patients. After all, we all want the same goals: high-quality care at the lowest level of care possible.

By understanding the basic concepts of medical necessity and our role in public health for the community, it strengthens the work with payers and the symbiotic role to help build effective and efficient practices hospital-wide while getting the care reimbursed. If you lean into learning this and collaborate with your payer partners, it makes the job much easier.

Denied claims are a burden to the healthcare system. Denials are generated when the care or level of service is thought to be not medically necessary or not meeting contracted guidelines. If you are finding trends with certain payers, denied inpatient claims, denials for post-acute care levels, work with the payers on smoothing out your processes.

Utilizing medical necessity criteria is important, but teaching your clinicians accurate documentation of the illness severity and required resource intensity is equally important. Payers pay the hospital. Payers will pay the hospital for the appropriate services when the medical care is necessary. If the care could be offered at a lower level, such as a post-acute facility or with home healthcare, then it is clinically best to transition to that lower level of care.

Making sure patients meet the criteria for the lower level of care is also crucial. Patients must have a skilled need for a skilled nursing (subacute rehabilitation) facility and must demonstrate the opportunity for progression and improvement to the prior baseline or a new baseline. Patients must also participate in their care to qualify for post-acute services. If you notice a payer having an inadequate network for post-acute services, discuss the opportunities with them directly. Compare with other payers to strengthen the pre- and post-hospitalization options.

Discharging from the hospital involves the multidisciplinary team. It is important to have the components of the discharge and which medications the patient will need, but also to link to outpatient care and ongoing disease management to prevent readmission to the hospital. Patients often need help with obtaining medications, transportation, or help with appointments for follow-up with primary and specialty care services. The more we help patients on discharge, the greater likelihood that patients will have a successful recovery to return to the prior baseline. Care of the patient requires attention to the biopsychosocial model of care. Evaluation of the patient's prehospital baseline is important, and evaluation of the new level of functionality and where the patient may discharge safely.

THE ROLE OF THE CMO

Hospitals are homes for the sick. However, hospitals are always open and ready to help patients. Thus, hospitals may also become utilized for safe shelter and access to food and medications. Patients often have dire home or social situations, including homelessness or increasing difficulty thriving in the home environment. It is important to identify the resources available in your community to help those who need help. Connect to the agencies providing home healthcare, medical equipment, transportation, caregiver services, reduced-cost services on a sliding scale. If you have community health centers or Federally Qualified Health Centers in the area, connect with them to provide referrals for patients. The stronger your connectedness to community resources and entities helping with pre- and post-hospital care, the smoother your patient transitions are in and out of the hospital.

Medical school teaches us about clinical problem-solving: gathering data in assessments to arrive at medical decision-making and treating patients to help them feel better and improve the quality of life. Now we must continue to learn about the new medical advancements while keeping up with the ever-changing rules about how to effectively deliver healthcare. Embracing constant change is one of the most important qualities as a clinical leader.

It is the role of the CMO to help clinicians understand how hospitals thrive in a challenging healthcare climate. Let's go back to a code blue called overhead in the hospital. Effectively running a code blue requires two things: (1) knowing the lifesaving algorithms and (2) leading a team to effectively implement the algorithm in the highest-pressure situation.

Being an effective CMO relies on the same concepts. It is important to understand the foundations of how hospitals operate and get paid, the specifics about your hospital or hospital system. It is equally as important to build your well-functioning team. Whether you are building a team, rebuilding a team, or joining an expert team, it is important to get to know your individual members. Work together to understand the reasons for the goals.

Before trying to motivate your team toward a goal, dive in to understand how the goal works and why it's important. Empower others about the mission. Building and retaining a high-quality workforce is more effective than trying to recruit a new one.

Hospitals will continue to be day and night, year-round homes for the sickest in our community. Hospitals are a vital part of the care continuum but are now in trouble with the many pressures of a high-cost operation, high denial rates due to the high costs, and so many services shifting to outpatient centers.

This is our chance to help hospitals. Be curious and be passionate. Learn about the new ways to thrive despite the changing healthcare climate. Negotiate with kindness. Build a team that works well together. Build a team that enjoys working through challenges. Then your team will come running to your hospital like an effective and life-saving code blue so that we may continue to save lives and help our communities.

CHAPTER 11

The CMO of a Medical Group

Christopher P. Hall, MD, MBA

THERE IS NO PHYSICIAN LEADER ROLE with as much variability as that of a CMO for a medical group given the wide array of ambulatory medical entities, from small physician-owned practices to large and complex groups, spanning the country, from small physician-owned practices to large and complex groups, with thousands of others in between these extremes.

If you were to teleport back to the turn of the century, you would find few of these entities had a formal CMO leader in place, but given the growth of groups in complexity, sophistication, and sheer size, an ever-increasing number have a devoted leader in this capacity. Changes in reimbursement models and contracts, along with new environmental challenges, have driven consolidation and thereby require ambulatory practices to invest in physician leadership.

These trends are likely to continue, demanding even more physicians are committed to leading their peers. In this chapter, we will examine the various requirements of the role, some characteristics of a strong CMO leader, as well as some differences from the hospital CMO.

MANAGING OTHERS

Almost certainly, medical group CMOs will be involved in the management of personnel, including physicians, other clinicians, and even non-clinical personnel. This involvement includes the hiring, supervising, and discharging of others. For many leaders, this will be the first time that they have been held accountable for other staff members, and they may not have the experience or skills to do this effortlessly. Regardless of the CMO's experience, it always requires effort and diligence.

It is often said that finding and hiring strong talent is one of the hallmarks of great leaders.[1] Today, retaining such talent is just as crucial. Acquiring physicians and other personnel is the largest investment many groups undertake. There is often pressure from many angles to hire that physician who is doing more than their share of call, the colleague with a friend seeking employment, or unused hours in the ambulatory surgery center.

The importance of being thorough throughout the hiring process cannot be understated. In hindsight, a soft yellow flag can easily turn into a major missed warning sign. The CMO should ensure that there is a careful process for verifying credentials, doing background checks, and verifying employment. This process must be applied uniformly and without bias. As painful as it can be to go without a critical clinical resource, one can multiply the anguish ten-fold when dismissing a physician colleague who was a poor fit.

CMOs can also be tasked with developing teams or committees. When doing so, it is beneficial to think broadly and inclusively to ensure that diverse experiences and voices are at the table. This is not only to ensure that all colleagues feel valued, but also to make teams stronger and help them come to better decisions.[2] Serving on these teams or committees can be a fantastic way to develop leaders or those with high leadership potential to get involved and gain experience. High-performing medical groups often have a regular cadence or practice of pulling in less-experienced physicians to various teams to provide them with the capability for other leadership positions.

Managing physicians and other clinicians typically includes some element of overseeing work schedules and productivity. It doesn't matter how big or small, simple or complex, every group must pay for support staff, meet the access needs of patients, and cover overhead expenses.

As was seen during the early years of the pandemic, most medical groups do not have access to large sums of cash needed to meet their operating costs for extended periods. Those entities that do have access to some funds are likely to have careful oversight. In most groups, there is a need to divide revenues equitably. All this requires fairness when it comes to productivity.

Many groups have enough scale and resources to establish a committee to oversee productivity and schedules. Typically, the CMO is a key component of this team. In other groups, the CMO may have to manage the physicians' production more directly. This could entail running reports, sharing data, leading conversations to reach an agreement, and even coaching those who are falling below the group's expectations.

Some medical groups base compensation on cash collections; others may leverage another productivity system, such as the work relative value unit (wRVU), which was established by CMS in 1992.[3] This system attempts to balance physician work effort, practice expenses, and malpractice expense.[4] Anyone aspiring to lead as a medical group CMO should familiarize themselves with this system. There are many resources, such as those through the Medical Group Management Association (MGMA),[5] with courses available on this topic.

An important aspect of managing schedules is ensuring access for patients. Patients must be able to be seen when it works for them. For too long, the medical office schedule has been organized largely for the benefit of the physicians and staff.

The success and survival of the group are also predicated on welcoming new patients and families to the practice. New patients are the equivalent of stem cells, highly valuable and helping the practice continually regenerate. Key specialties such as obstetrics, pediatrics, family medicine, urgent care, and others should always maintain a friendly face at the front door. They are most likely to see the new mother, baby, or family that forms the essential base of their ever-expanding lives.

The CMO and other leaders, such as managers and directors, should always be advocates for bringing new patients into the fold. It may be convenient to limit hours, access, and panels, but the best interest of the group is to be relentlessly expanding, both in lives covered and access to care. The medical group CMO needs to be a principal promoter of a welcoming culture.

No other area of responsibility can be as rewarding or wearying as that of addressing personnel and, especially, behavioral issues. A medical group CMO will undoubtedly be called to assist in coaching others, whether it be physicians, other clinicians, or other roles in the group. It is perhaps the single most important aspect of the role.

When personnel issues go unchecked, they can wreak havoc on the organization, introduce risk, cause harm, and sour group culture. When resolution goes well, it can be incredibly rewarding for all parties and create a positive history and sense of loyalty that contributes to psychological safety among group members. When those involved cannot recognize concerns, agree on the causes, or find any common ground for understanding, it can be grueling and exhausting.

Much can be done to mitigate some of the pain of essential work. First, become skilled at providing feedback. In everyday life, there are millions of opportunities to practice and learn; seize them. It is important to emphasize the positive and make sure feedback is direct and specific. In lieu of "you did a great job in that meeting," something like "I really appreciated how you organized the agenda, got it out in advance, and made certain that you heard from everyone at the table" may be more efficacious and uplifting.

Kim Scott makes a compelling argument for the importance of feedback. She points out that it is the moral obligation of the boss to criticize fairly and constructively.[6] Her book *Radical Candor* is a valuable resource for learning how to do this well. It is indispensable for a CMO to be an expert at feedback.

CMOs must be able to triage what can be accomplished with a quick chat, perhaps over a cup of coffee, and what necessitates a more formal setting, possibly with another leader joining in. Typically, if the issue is arising for the first time, isn't a major violation of group standards or policy, and doesn't involve significant harm to another party, the informal approach is a good place to start.

It is always necessary to recap with some form of documentation. For example, "Thanks for meeting with me regarding chart closure. I appreciate that you are going to put in some extra time to get them completed within our 24-hour rule. I know that can be difficult. Let me know if you need any support or need to follow up." The summary doesn't need to be exhaustive, but there needs to be some record of the conversation.

At times, a concerning issue involves strong emotions, differing views, and even significant risks to one party or possibly both. When that is the case, it is time for a crucial conversation. It would be impossible to summarize everything a CMO needs to know in short order, but here are a few key points.

Preparation is always helpful; try to learn as much as possible in advance. Be sure to look at situations from other points of view. Consider if having another leader or party present will keep things fair and balanced.

It might be helpful to address issues in more than one conversation by first introducing the concern and hearing the opposing thoughts on the matter. Then, come back together to problem solve and develop a plan. Not everything can or should be solved in a single meeting.

Once the conversation(s) have occurred, make sure to document what was said, providing a copy to all involved while officially and securely recording the concern, discussion, and plan. Nothing is more frustrating than learning of a problem, with a mention of "it has been going on forever," and finding no documentation as to what has been done or attempted. Almost always, it pays to check back on the topic, and if it is of significant consequence, come to an agreement to do so regularly until some objectives are met.

Most CMOs find it beneficial to undertake formal training on this topic, and there are many options. Some organizations are dedicated to this training and offer resources, such as AAPL.[7]

Finally, be persistent. If the concern is substantial enough to come together to address it once, don't let it go before a satisfactory resolution is met. Unresolved issues can weigh on all parties and be a detriment to the overall functioning of a group.

FINDING NEEDED SUPPORT

As mentioned earlier, managing physicians and other providers can be wearing. One potential source of strength for the ambulatory CMO can be other experienced colleagues. In many medical groups, there are at least a few and possibly several physicians who have served in leadership roles previously or, at least, have served on the board of directors or in similar roles. It is wise to bring them together regularly to discuss topics of concern to gain input, provide guidance, and serve as a sounding board for ideas. They may also occupy additional roles, such as mentoring colleagues, leading *ad hoc* committees, or even attending crucial conversations as a third party.

As with all teams, it is good to be inclusive and ensure that diverse voices and experiences are well-represented. Gone should be the days when leaders were essentially a monoculture. The medical group CMO role can be a lonely one; having a supportive bench of experienced colleagues can be both reassuring and a source of strength.

Another source of support can be those who have been elevated into positions of responsibility, such as medical directors, department chairs, and others in similar roles. The ambulatory CMO is often accountable for these positions, and they can be helpful in leading important service areas closer to patient care.

Of course, each ambulatory entity will vary in the number and scope of these frontline physician leaders, but they often help manage many important domains of care. For example, medical directors are commonly empowered to lead their colleagues in productivity, quality of outcomes, patient safety event reviews, and addressing performance concerns. They also can assist in hiring and advancing colleagues.

Notably, medical directors can guide improvement initiatives, assist with staff relations, and help form a leadership team. Medical directors and similar roles provide a great reservoir of developing leaders, many of whom can be considered as potential succession candidates, especially since a typical CMO will serve less than five years.[8]

High-performing developing leaders should be considered for medical director roles. It may be helpful to avoid having a single physician serve in the same role for many years, thereby preventing others from gaining essential experience. An additional ally is a dyad leadership partner. Dyads are usually two leaders who form a partnership and work closely together, such as a physician leader and an administrator. In the medical group, it is commonly the CMO, chief nursing officer (CNO), or another nurse leader.

The CMO may help set the tone for the group, lead conversations with clinicians, and directly manage other physicians such as medical directors. The CNO will typically perform similar duties for the nursing teams, technical staff, and others but also lead the implementation or operationalization of various initiatives. Again, the CMO road can be isolating; it is best to develop relationships with others who can serve as allies.

QUALITY/SAFETY

Like the hospital CMO, the physician leader of the medical group is first and foremost concerned with patient safety and quality of care. It is critical to establish a system that closely monitors for safety events that have the potential to harm patients. Common outpatient events include those related to medication administration, wrong patient identification (including lost or mislabeled lab specimens), or, depending on the scope of practice, adverse effects of various procedures such as allergy injections, contrast media infusions, or medication delivery.

Medical groups should be able to capture these events, catalog them, and analyze the data, looking for trends and opportunities to improve the care delivery system. For serious safety events, such as a wrong site procedure or medication error with severe harm or death, the CMO should be trained and skilled in leading a root cause analysis, identifying latent roots that can be addressed to prevent the event from occurring again in the future.

It is also imperative to establish a culture of psychological safety, encouraging all clinicians and staff to speak up for safety. The ambulatory environment depends on highly effective teams, and those teams must have a feeling of safety that allows individual members to speak up when needed. The CMO, along with the CNO and others, is a key leader in creating a culture that provides for psychological safety.

In the ambulatory setting, all staff members must be willing to identify mistakes and, especially, self-disclose errors.[9] Think about the complexity of the current pediatric immunization schedule. Even with extensive training and experience, it can be difficult to provide the right product at the right time. Given the millions of immunizations provided yearly in the United States, it would be easy for a nurse to avoid disclosing the error to other team members or even the patient and family members.

Errors must be examined from a process and system lens, identifying actions that can be put in place to prevent the event in the future. The CMO has a responsibility to set the expectation that mistakes will occur and that they must be identified, shared, and, hopefully, learned from to reduce harm both in that single event and going forward.

The CMO is charged with ensuring that the quality of care meets patients' expectations and is aligned with the prevailing standard of care. Key metrics need to be tracked — ideally, down to the specialty level — to ensure that patients are receiving appropriate care. CMOs, in partnership with other leaders such as medical directors and department chairs, should review the results of targeted metrics regularly.

It is important not to just admire the results but to have an inquiring and open mind to causality when reviewing the data. The key process is sustained quality improvement, always working to improve our care delivery while meeting patients' expectations. This will be discussed a bit more later in this chapter. One useful source of quality measures comes from the National Committee on Quality Assurance,[10] an organization founded in the early 1990s to improve the care that is delivered. Many health plans use the HEDIS (Healthcare Effectiveness Data and Information Set) to gauge the overall care being delivered. There are more than 90 measures available across a handful of domains. Focus areas include efficacy, access to care, utilization, and the care experience. Focusing on the HEDIS measures will allow a medical group to align with the interests of major payers.

Some of these measures may be built into the group's electronic medical record (EMR) to facilitate measurement, recording, and improvement. There are also vendors who offer services to assist with measurement and progression. In the current healthcare market, it is not enough to think that a group is providing diligent care; it must be demonstrated through measurement, sharing, and reporting.

As mentioned above, it is not enough to see and review results. It is critical that key outcomes are identified for opportunity and then followed through with quantifiable improvement. In fact, quality improvement initiatives are a fantastic chance to gain valuable leadership experience. There are many improvement methodologies with various advantages and, typically, some drawbacks; the important point is to take intentional steps to learn at least one. This can be initially accomplished by working alongside a more experienced leader and eventually by undertaking a more structured education.

There are many models for improvement, but a few well-known ones in healthcare are Lean, Six Sigma,[11] and IHI's Model for Improvement.[12] The most key point is to learn at least one well, as it will serve a purpose in improvement work no matter what role a developing leader occupies. Much like medicine, the science underlying improvement makes the practice thereof much more reliable and apt to persist.

Alongside the quality and safety of care sits the actual experience enjoyed by the patient. In reviewing the Triple Aim, the experience of the care is closely aligned with the quality and safety, yielding a triangle when one includes the health of a population and the per capita cost.[13] The CMO, in partnership with other leaders such as the CNO, is a strong advocate for the patient. Ideally, the care environment and processes are thoughtfully designed with the patient in mind.

Many medical groups pull for the voice of the patient through advisory panels, focus groups, surveys, and deliberate searches for feedback. This allows patients to have more proactive input and can also identify concerns before they become a liability to the organization. If those aren't reason enough, many payers expect some form of patient experience reporting. Strong medical group CMOs never neglect the input of the patient in their work.

BUSINESS MANAGEMENT

Business management can be foreign territory for many physicians. There are areas, such as finance, which may be unfamiliar and require significant attention, and others that may help satisfy the urge to build or develop.

The CMO often serves on a team to develop strategic plans or at least outline some key initiatives. In the past, many groups relied on long-term plans, potentially outlining new initiatives over 5–10 years. Given the many uncertainties in the healthcare market today, most groups are planning not as far ahead. However, programmatic and service line development can be a source of fulfillment for many CMOs.

CMOs often are asked or want to look at the group's clinical portfolio and determine what needs to expand, potential new offerings, and, at times, what should be pruned. Unless a group has secure cash reserves and a culture of taking risks, it is prudent to be thoughtful and reflective in pursuing new ventures. It's not that they shouldn't be done, but that the impacts should be examined from all angles and include stakeholders that can help provide input and expertise in putting the plan together.

Most projects should have a business plan or *pro forma* budget that provides some forecast of the financial benefit. The most fastidious leaders will want to look back on these financial estimates periodically to check on the estimates, as they can serve to inform the planning process going forward.

Unless a physician leader is fortunate to have relevant business experience, most will need to acquire it while serving in a leadership role. Healthcare accounting is a difficult and confusing topic with extremely complex elements. Patients are billed one thing, contractual write-offs are another, and the resulting dollars collected can appear like a result of a Byzantine labyrinth. To make matters worse, the clinicians may be paid based on cash collections, wRVUs, or some other method. Having a compensation system that physicians cannot follow can sow distrust with the leadership.

The CMO frequently serves as a connection between clinicians and the business team. Fortunately, most groups have a CFO or, at least, a business manager who can serve as an ally and great source of information. It is imperative for the CMO to spend time with them and learn the system that is in place. It should be understood by the leader, and, in turn, they must be able to explain it to their colleagues.

A good practice is to sit with the finance leader monthly to understand the finances, productivity, and trends. Over time, a physician leader will gain much of the comprehension required to be a resource to their constituents. It is an advantage to gain advanced finance education through courses, seminars, or even a master's degree in business. This is particularly true for larger, more complicated entities that may have multiple service lines, ventures, or business units.

Documentation and coding are essential functions, especially as the early intent of helping to communicate health information for colleagues has become so intricately tied to billing, reimbursement, and even quality metrics. The medical group CMO will certainly benefit from having some advanced knowledge on the topic. In small groups, they may need to function as a principal expert. Larger groups likely have internal resources that can support these functions. However, the CMO will still be a primary driver of activities. Most CMOs should seek advanced education in coding and documentation; there are many resources available to facilitate this training.

Medical groups can have a wide variety of malpractice insurance arrangements. Some groups purchase coverage directly through an insurer; some may be self-insured. The CMO needs to have a good understanding of the malpractice configuration. Given the alignment between patient safety, risk management, and malpractice experience, there is a great opportunity to undertake initiatives that reduce harm to patients and conserve financial resources. To have an effective program, it is necessary to have trended patient safety data, looking for both successes to celebrate and opportunities to improve.

Contracts are an important area that may not receive a lot of attention — that is, until something doesn't go well with a contract or there is a lack of a contract where one would have been helpful to clarify expectations and responsibilities. It pays to understand contracts and to learn how they should be written, what elements to include, and what to avoid.

In the past, many contracts were verbal agreements by two well-meaning representatives, but in healthcare today, almost all contracts are written. A good rule is that if the thought occurs that you might need a contract, then it is beneficial to put one in place. Contracts are a good way to establish expectations for each party, as well as the expected time frame, compensation, and any important performance metrics, which can often be in an addendum.

There may be an attorney at the disposal of the group or on staff who can assist with the language. Some common contracts will have a template that can be utilized to save time. For example, most groups will use a common employment contract for all physicians. There may be a contract for the CMO role, certain professional services agreements, and for common roles such as medical directors.

SUMMARY

The medical group shares several similarities with that on the acute side. Both must have a steady hand, excel at emotional intelligence, and thoughtfully serve alongside their colleagues. They make excellent use of humble inquiry and seek to understand. Each must go on the gemba to listen, see, and hear.

With that, there are several differences in the role. Even though the medical group will likely have some important regulatory requirements, it is typically much smaller in scale and scope with respect to the acute side. Another enormous difference is the constituencies. The medical group CMO may be elected or chosen in some way by their colleagues. They often serve both at the head and alongside their peers. The hospital CMO is a member of management and typically is accountable for the medical staff functions. Oversight of the medical staff department, various meetings, and elected leaders requires significant effort.

In general, a CMO leading an ambulatory group typically has more alignment with their constituents. To take that a step further, many medical groups function like a large, complex family, whereas a hospital is often a small town or city with disparate voices, stakeholders, and competing interests.

Leading physicians as a CMO requires determination, grit, and persistence. There are always countless competing interests and never enough hours in the day. At the end of the day, there is always work on the desk and at least one more call to do. Still, CMOs persevere. The role is critical to the success of the organization and in helping to deliver high-quality care to patients.

It is important for CMOs to use small successes to refill their reservoir of energy. It is also critical to care for themselves. The CMO role is a long grind; a strong physician leader needs to pace and care for themself. It is important to take time for self-reflection, meditation, exercise, or whatever helps them recharge and re-energize. There will always be more to do, but if a leader is not there, the group will suffer a huge loss. Never neglect oneself.

The medical group CMO will be leading a lot of exciting and crucial changes. In the current healthcare market, hospitals are becoming challenging cost centers. Numerous acute facilities are in duress and struggling mightily to reduce their overhead expense. The medical groups are struggling but are in a much better position for potential solutions.

Ambulatory groups have many patient interactions compared to hospitals, and patients have stronger loyalty to their office clinicians. Medical groups also are forming strong alliances with payers in unique arrangements; indeed, many groups are quite attractive for the number of lives for which they are accountable. These cooperative relationships may bring new capital to this space as well as new technological solutions.

Ambulatory groups have always been recognized for their strong ownership of the patient in the form of the medical home model, but now, there is a broader acceptance of this approach beyond primary care to vital specialty care as well. Leading this work as a CMO is sure to be challenging, though exciting.

There is enormous potential for good to come from these challenges. It is incumbent upon our developing physician leaders to step into the medical group CMO role with new, creative, and provocative solutions to steer medical groups through this demanding time.

REFERENCES

1. Renteria R. New Leaders, Here's How to Hire a Top Talent. *Harvard Business Review.* January 2, 2024.

2. Rock D, Grant H. Why Diverse Teams Are Smarter. *Harvard Business Review*. November 4, 2016.

3. Spragens LH, Silvers A. Everything You Always Wanted to Know About RVUs But Were Afraid to Ask. Center to Advance Palliative Care. February 28, 2023. https://www.capc.org/blog/everything-you-always-wanted-to-know-about-rvus -but-were-afraid-to-ask/

4. Reinhardt UE. How Medicare Pays Physicians. The New York Times. December 3, 2010. https://archive.nytimes.com/economix.blogs.nytimes.com/2010/12/03/ how-medicare-pays-physicians/

5. Medical Group Management Association. Homepage. mgma.com.

6. Scott K. *Radical Candor*. New York: St. Martin's Press; 2019.

7. American Association for Physician Leadership. Homepage. physicianleaders.org.

8. Resnick A. Keys to Success as a Chief Medical Officer: Navigating the "Toughest Job in Healthcare." Chartis blog. July 26, 2023. https://www.chartis.com/insights/ keys-success-chief-medical-officer-navigating-toughest-job-healthcare

9. Gallo A. What Is Psychological Safety? *Harvard Business Review*. February 15, 2023.

10. NCQA. About NCQA. https://www.ncqa.org/about-ncqa/

11. Six Sigma. Understanding the Basics – Lean Process Improvement. Six Sigma. February 21, 2017. https://www.6sigma.us/six-sigma-articles/understanding- basics-lean-process-improvement/

12. Institute for Healthcare Improvement. How to Improve: Model for Improvement. IHI. https://www.ihi.org/resources/how-to-improve

13. Institute for Healthcare Improvement. Triple Aim and Population Health. IHI. https://www.ihi.org/improvement-areas/triple-aim-population-health

CHAPTER 12

The CMO of a Health Plan

Michael J. Menen, MD

A HEALTH PLAN CHIEF MEDICAL OFFICER (CMO) was traditionally responsible for overseeing only the medical aspects of a health plan, such as medical policy and utilization management. The role of the CMO in health plans has evolved significantly over the years due to the rapidly changing healthcare landscape. Innovations and trends in this role have been driven by the need for more integrated and patient-centered care, advancements in medical and business technology, and the increasing complexity of health plan operations.

Additionally, most CMOs today have significant business acumen, unlike the traditional CMO, who was principally a medical expert with decent communications skills. The CMO now plays a key role in strategic planning and the development of clinical initiatives aimed at improving healthcare outcomes, patient and provider experience, and cost-efficiency.

Before elaborating on the role of a health plan CMO, it is important to describe what a health plan is and how it operates. Understanding this will put the role in context and explain why CMOs have certain responsibilities and where they can make the most impact.

DEFINING A HEALTH PLAN

A health plan is simply a package of healthcare coverage benefits that use a particular network (e.g., HMO, PPO) to deliver services within a defined service area. In practice, a health plan is but one of many "products" and services provided by an insurance company. Many draw a distinction between a health plan and an insurance company, but practically speaking, a health plan CMO works for an insurance company.

Insurance companies are not really in the business of providing care, even if they employ clinicians. They are in the business of managing and administering healthcare benefits, which involves risk assessment, underwriting, and network contracting.

Claims management is a fundamental part of the operation of a health insurance company. Health plan CMOs may provide clinical direction to those ensuring that the services claimed to have been rendered are covered and meet the established guidelines and policy terms. Nurses and coders, under the direction of medical directors, verify the diagnosis, treatment, and costs associated with the claim.

As the principal liaison between the provider and insurance company, a health plan CMO may be called on to resolve specific issues providers have regarding reimbursement or coverage for a particular service.

Claims processing and validation is a fundamental method by which insurance companies control their expenses and reduce fraudulent or unnecessary claims, thus ensuring financial viability. Claims processing is an enormous task. Billions of claims are submitted, and trillions of dollars are exchanged annually involving thousands of disparate healthcare systems. Errors are, not surprisingly, rampant in this antiquated and byzantine compensation system.

Health insurance companies also focus on community outreach, customer service, and support. For a CMO, this means educating policyholders about their health and benefits, and helping them navigate the healthcare system.

Health and wellness programs, such as preventive care initiatives and discounts on gym memberships, are increasingly common services aimed at promoting healthier lifestyles among policyholders. As a health plan CMO, you might perform a variety of tasks to move these efforts forward, from sponsoring a vaccination drive at a school to creating more general programs for some of the plan's clients.

These services are attractive to buyers of health insurance (i.e., employers), but are also useful in mitigating risk and minimizing the development and progression of illness. In addition to education, CMOs validate the medical information disseminated to policyholders and determine the criteria of wellness benchmarks that translate into discounts for policyholders.

CMOs may play a role in developing provider and other contracts. Many considerations are factored into these contracts: obligation to provide services, competition with other payers, client preferences (usually a commercial or government entity), federal and state regulations, outcome metrics, demographics, and a host of other factors.

The diversity of issues and variability of resources is the reason these contracts are so complex. Some familiar variables might be the number of charts subject to audit, length of stay or outlier payment considerations, and exclusivity (often in exchange for preferred rates). CMOs may be involved in these negotiations and will certainly be expected to explain the provisions of these contracts to providers and enforce them within the networks they oversee.

In addition to administering health benefits, insurance companies are financial institutions; investing the premiums they receive is one of their primary operations. Insurance companies have large investment portfolios that help the insurer maintain sufficient reserves to pay claims, generate profit, and ensure long-term stability. Effective investment management is crucial for insurance companies to maintain financial stability and meet the needs of policyholders as well as stockholders.

Insurance companies often provide data and analytics services, pharmacy services, population health programs, and primary and secondary care. They also manage and provide a variety of healthcare operations services as "third-party administrators." In this case, the insurance company is not providing coverage or taking on risk.

THE ROLE OF THE CMO

A health plan CMO may work in only one of these sectors or might touch multiple or even all of them. Certainly, CMOs must deal with many aspects of the insurance business, regardless of the role they occupy. Thus, the ability to collaborate effectively with other departments is crucial for the overall success and effectiveness of the organization and the CMO. Even if a CMO and other leaders have the same goals, compromises often are necessary to realize initiatives and to meet the organization's overall goals.

Each department brings its unique perspective, expertise, and resources to the table. Only by understanding what motivates different departments can a CMO organize a consensus and develop integrated solutions that will meet the needs of all stakeholders. By sharing information and resources across departments, the inevitable redundancies can be minimized, and tasks can be streamlined.

For instance, if the medical management department has a list of high-risk members, collaborating with the customer service department can ensure that these members receive personalized attention and support that may decrease their utilization of the emergency room. Likewise, collaborating with the finance department can enable accurate budgeting and cost-effective decision-making, and ensure innovations and projects enjoy the financial support needed to get off the ground.

This collaboration also extends to external stakeholders. As a bridge between healthcare professionals and insurance companies, CMOs must collaborate with healthcare providers, hospitals, and clinics to establish and maintain partnerships that support the health plan's goals. The CMO may be involved in negotiating contracts, monitoring provider performance, and addressing any concerns or issues that arise.

As a key member of a health plan's leadership team, CMOs analyze healthcare utilization data, identify trends, and implement strategies to address any gaps in care. This collaborative relationship ensures a strong network of healthcare providers who can deliver high-quality care to the health plan members. Frequently, this partnership involves differences of opinion; therefore, a CMO's ability to diplomatically negotiate solutions is an important part of the job.

I want to specifically mention government and media relations. As a health plan CMO, you will be expected to interact with public officials, regulators, and legislators on a local level, and often will find yourself on committees addressing some issue or another. Health plans typically play a key role in the local well-being of the community and the CMO's involvement reflects that responsibility.

CMOs often represent the health plan, particularly in the local community. The ability to speak to and engage community members is a key skill. The same applies at a national level, as the CMO will often set the clinical tone for a company and address the contemporaneous issues that arise in the media. At the very least, ensuring that company policies and practices align with the public interests as they evolve is imperative.

A key aspect of the CMO's role is to provide medical expertise and guidance. CMOs must stay up to date with current medical knowledge, research, best practices, and emerging technologies to ensure that the health plan's policies and procedures align with evidence-based guidelines and processes that promote streamlined care delivery and optimized utilization of resources.

CMOs are expected to address a variety of medical issues. In other words, CMOs are not valuable just because of their knowledge, but also their ability to learn and educate non-clinical departments about other specialties. For example, a cardiologist may need to learn about podiatry.

A CMO plays a pivotal role in addressing population health management. With a focus on preventive care and chronic disease management, the CMO helps develop programs and initiatives to promote healthier lifestyles and improve overall population health outcomes. By analyzing population health data, identifying high-risk individuals, and implementing targeted interventions, the CMO can reduce healthcare costs, improve patient satisfaction, and enhance the health and well-being of the plan's members.

KEY CMO RESPONSIBILITIES

Successful CMOs have a variety of qualifications and skills to effectively execute their responsibilities. Their responsibilities encompass a wide range of tasks, focusing on strategic planning, medical management, policy development, and provider engagement. Five key responsibilities of a health plan CMO include:

1. **Strategic planning**: One of the primary responsibilities of a health plan CMO is to develop and implement strategic plans. This includes setting medical goals and objectives, identifying areas for improvement, and formulating strategies to enhance patient care outcomes. The CMO must be knowledgeable about current healthcare trends, research, and advancements to ensure the health plan remains innovative and responsive to the evolving needs of its members.

2. **Medical management**: CMOs may oversee medical management activities within the health plan. This involves collaborating with various departments to develop care management programs, utilization management policies, quality improvement initiatives, and clinical guidelines. The CMO ensures that these programs and policies are evidence-based, cost-effective, and aligned with industry standards to achieve the best outcomes for patients. On a local level, a CMO is charged with getting buy-in, managing issues and expectations, monitoring outcomes, and providing feedback.

3. **Policy development and adherence**: Policy development is an essential function within an insurance company and health plan. A

large team that includes stakeholders from many areas of the organization is typically involved in the development of policies. The CMO plays a vital role in policy development, providing clinical insight and guidance. The CMO must collaborate closely with key stakeholders, such as the compliance and legal departments, administration, and others to ensure that policies and procedures are up to date and in line with industry standards.

Importantly, a principal responsibility of a CMO, at a more local level, is to ensure that providers, and occasionally members, understand and adhere to these policies, thereby ensuring the delivery of safe and high-quality healthcare services.

4. **Provider engagement**: Maintaining effective relationships with healthcare providers is crucial for the success of the health plan. The CMO takes a lead role in engaging with network providers, developing strategic partnerships, and fostering collaborative relationships. This involves conducting regular meetings, forums, and conferences to address provider concerns, communicate medical policies, and seek input for the development and improvement of the health plan's programs and initiatives. Provider engagement also ensures that members have access to a broad network of high-quality providers and services.

5. **Clinical oversight and quality improvement**: The CMO is responsible for providing clinical oversight to ensure the quality and safety of care provided to health plan members. They collaborate with clinical staff and quality improvement teams to develop programs that monitor and evaluate the performance of providers and healthcare facilities. Regular audits, performance reviews, and data analysis help identify areas for improvement and implement appropriate actions to enhance the overall quality of care.

The CMO also plays a critical role in promoting patient safety and advocating for evidence-based practices that reduce medical errors and improve outcomes.

TRAINING AND EXPERIENCE

In addition to medical qualifications, a CMO should have experience in the healthcare industry. Advanced training in a relevant field, such as healthcare management or health informatics, while not mandatory, can be beneficial. This may include several years of clinical practice, preferably in leadership positions, where they have developed expertise in managing patient care, healthcare quality, and clinical guidelines. Experience working with health plans, insurance companies, or managed care organizations is highly valued, as it provides an understanding of the intricacies and challenges of healthcare delivery within these systems.

A CMO should have a record of effectively leading and managing teams. The importance of strong interpersonal skills and the ability to build relationships with both internal and external stakeholders cannot be overstated. CMOs must be able to effectively communicate with various stakeholders, including executives, regulators, and policymakers. The ability to clearly articulate complex medical concepts and describe a compelling vision is essential in driving positive change within the organization.

A CMO, like most executives within a large organization, must lead without having authority over all components of an issue. Diplomacy, persuasion, and negotiation skills are important when collaborating with partners, since without them you will not be able to advance your agenda.

An understanding of health plan operations and the regulatory environment is important. A CMO should be knowledgeable about health insurance coverage, payment models, and reimbursement strategies. Familiarity with relevant laws and regulations, such as the Affordable Care Act (ACA) and the Centers for Medicare and Medicaid Services (CMS) regulations, is crucial to ensure compliance and navigate the complex healthcare landscape.

Strong strategic thinking and decision-making abilities are essential to guide the health plan's medical policies, programs, and initiatives. Analytical and critical thinking skills are necessary for the CMO to evaluate healthcare data, identify opportunities for improvement, and develop strategies, supported by data, to enhance the health plan's performance.

A CMO should have experience utilizing healthcare analytics and data systems to track and measure outcomes, identify trends, and make data-driven decisions. The CMO should be comfortable using and delivering this data in presentations that support their initiatives.

Given the increasing importance of technology in healthcare, a CMO should have proficiency in health information technology (HIT) and familiarity with electronic health records (EHRs), health information exchange

(HIE), and other healthcare software systems. They should be well-versed in leveraging digital tools to improve patient care, population health management, and care coordination.

COMMON CHALLENGES

Being a health plan CMO is a challenge that requires constant adaptation. One major challenge health plan CMOs face is the ever-increasing cost of healthcare. They must find ways to balance the need for cost containment with the provision of high-quality care to members. This requires careful analysis of data, monitoring of utilization patterns, and implementation of effective cost-saving measures.

On a practical and more local level, CMOs must address specific provider and member situations, including the number of "heads in beds," lengths of stay, outlier patients, and other medical necessity issues. It is routine to engage with UM staff, medical directors, and other stakeholders to manage costs and promote cost savings initiatives that focus on getting patients to the best and most cost-effective place for care.

Another challenge is the complexity of healthcare regulations and policies. CMOs must stay updated with the constantly changing regulatory requirements. They need to adapt their operations and policies accordingly to ensure compliance, which can be a daunting task. Failure to comply with regulations can have serious legal and financial implications for the health plan.

Managing provider networks is a particular challenge for CMOs. They must ensure that the network is robust, inclusive, and comprised of high-quality healthcare providers. This involves negotiating contracts with providers, evaluating their performance, and addressing any concerns or issues that arise.

CMOs regularly manage the inevitable flux of groups going into or out of network and assist members by providing alternate providers when called for. Reasons may be the absence of a service within a particular network (ex., specific and unusual procedures) or due to conflicts that arise between providers and members. Maintaining good relationships with providers is crucial for delivering the best care to the plan's members.

The increasing prevalence of chronic diseases is also a challenge for CMOs. They must develop strategies to effectively manage chronic conditions and promote preventive care to improve health outcomes and reduce healthcare costs. This involves working with care management teams, developing care pathways, and implementing programs, including digital solutions where applicable, to support members in managing their health.

While health plans generate vast amounts of data, integrating and utilizing technology effectively can be challenging due to system complexities, interoperability issues, and data security concerns.

Another important aspect of a CMO's leadership strategy is establishing a culture of continuous improvement. This involves promoting a learning environment where healthcare professionals feel encouraged to identify areas for enhancement and implement evidence-based practices. By embracing a mindset of constant growth and innovation, the CMO can drive positive change internally, resulting in improved patient outcomes and member satisfaction.

Moreover, the CMO should actively engage in quality improvement initiatives, leveraging data analytics and performance metrics to identify areas of opportunity and track the effectiveness of interventions.

TRENDS IN HEALTH PLAN CMO ROLES

To stay ahead in the ever-evolving healthcare industry, CMOs must be aware of the latest innovations and trends. One major innovation in health plan CMO roles is the emphasis on value-based care. CMOs are now responsible for implementing strategies to ensure that healthcare services are of high quality and affordable and improve patient outcomes. They work closely with providers and healthcare networks to develop alternative payment models and promote care coordination. This shift has resulted in a stronger focus on population health management, preventive care, and chronic disease management.

Another trend in health plan CMO roles is the integration of technology and data analytics. CMOs are leveraging advanced analytics and artificial intelligence to improve decision-making and identify opportunities for cost savings and efficiency; digital health tools and telemedicine have become essential in delivering care, and CMOs are responsible for integrating these technologies into health plan offerings.

The emergence of consumerism in healthcare has also influenced the CMO's role in health plans. CMOs are increasingly involved in developing and implementing consumer engagement strategies to improve member satisfaction and promote preventive care. They work with marketing teams to create personalized health management programs and tools, digital and otherwise, and various programs that empower individuals to take control of their health. CMOs are also responsible for ensuring transparency in quality and helping members with information to make informed decisions about their care.

Social determinants of health are at the forefront in health plan CMO roles. Health plans recognize that social factors, such as education, housing, and access to nutritious food, significantly affect health outcomes. CMOs must collaborate with community organizations and social services to address these determinants and develop initiatives that support vulnerable populations. CMOs are also responsible for promoting health equity and reducing disparities in healthcare access and outcomes.

Finally, the CMO's role in health plans has expanded to include advocacy and policy development. CMOs now play a vital role in shaping healthcare policies that impact their members and the overall health system. They engage with key stakeholders, such as government agencies, advocacy groups, and professional associations to influence policy decisions and advocate for changes that improve patient care and outcomes.

STEPS TO A THRIVING CAREER

Building a successful career as a health plan CMO requires a combination of leadership skills, medical expertise, and a deep understanding of the healthcare landscape. Here are some key steps that can help a clinician achieve a thriving career in this role.

1. **Achieving medical excellence is crucial**. This can be accomplished by pursuing continuous education, staying up to date with the latest medical advancements, and regularly engaging in professional development activities. CMOs must have a deep understanding of clinical guidelines, evidence-based medicine, and healthcare quality metrics. Maintaining a strong clinical foundation is essential for ensuring the delivery of high-quality care to the members of the health plan.

2. **Effective leadership and managerial skills are paramount**. The ability to lead a team, collaborate with other executives and stakeholders, and make informed decisions is vital in this role. CMOs should inspire their teams to work toward common goals, foster a culture of innovation, and promote interdisciplinary collaboration. Effective communication and conflict resolution skills are also essential to navigating complex healthcare environments and building strong partnerships with providers and other stakeholders.

3. **In addition to medical and leadership skills, a strong business acumen is necessary.** CMOs should develop a deep understanding of the health plan's financial performance, utilization patterns, and market dynamics. This knowledge allows them to make data-driven decisions that contribute to the plan's success and sustainability. They should also be adept at interpreting and applying healthcare policies and regulations to ensure compliance and optimize the plan's operations.

4. **Building a successful career as a CMO involves cultivating strong relationships with key stakeholders within and outside the organization.** Building trust and credibility with fellow executives, providers, and regulatory bodies is essential for a CMO's effectiveness in implementing strategic initiatives and driving positive outcomes. This can be achieved through active engagement in professional networks, attending conferences, and participating in industry events. Additionally, staying abreast of current healthcare trends and sharing thought leadership can enhance a CMOs reputation and contribute to career growth.

Ethical considerations play a significant role in a CMO's decision-making process. Ethical challenges CMOs face include conflicts of interest, resource allocation, and patient privacy. CMOs are typically the primary advocates for patient-centered care, health equity, and evidence-based medicine.

It is the CMOs responsibility to ensure equal access to healthcare services for all members. This requires making fair and just decisions, and making sure health plans consider factors such as the patient's medical needs and financial limitations. A CMO must effectively balance providing appropriate care with the mindful allocation of limited resources.

A CMO must foster a culture of adherence to professional ethical standards within the organization. Inherent in the role of the health plan CMO is optimizing healthcare outcomes in the face of conflicting interests.

A CMO's decisions must consistently prioritize what is best for patients and the community, void of personal or financial influences. To achieve this, it is crucial for the CMO to maintain objectivity and transparency throughout their decision-making process, being mindful of and addressing any potential conflicts that may arise. By upholding these fundamental ethical principles, the CMO can foster trust among stakeholders while upholding integrity within their health plan's operations.

THE INDISPENSABLE HEALTH PLAN CMO

The role of a health plan CMO is indispensable in today's healthcare environment. From ensuring evidence-based guidelines to promoting collaboration between healthcare providers and insurance companies, the CMO is instrumental in driving the success of a health plan. By focusing on quality care, cost-effectiveness, and overall population health improvement, the CMO contributes to the achievement of better health outcomes for plan members.

To build a successful career as a health plan CMO, one must acquire medical expertise, develop leadership and management skills, possess a strong business acumen, and cultivate relationships with key stakeholders. By continuously investing in professional growth and staying adaptable to the evolving healthcare landscape, individuals can thrive in this influential position, improving the health outcomes for the members of the health plan.

Some think that leaving medical practice to work with an insurance company is like sleeping with the enemy. It is not. A health plan CMO has an opportunity to represent what the ideal care for patients is, to advocate for the right care, and to influence the way health plans deliver care to thousands if not millions of people. The role can bring out the best a clinician has to offer: motivational speaking, strategic thinking, business acumen, negotiation, and more.

CHAPTER 13

The CMO of a Health System

Amy L. Compton-Phillips, MD

BEFORE COVID PROVED ME WRONG, I thought the hardest year of my career would be the one when I transitioned from a regional leadership to a system-level leadership role. I was with Kaiser Permanente in the Mid-Atlantic States region centered around the Baltimore-Washington area.

I had taken the path into leadership most physicians follow: being a well-respected front-line clinician and good citizen of the medical group, being willing to work hard and listen to others, and then getting tapped on the shoulder to take on additional responsibilities. I was lucky to be part of an organization that invested in professional development, giving us access to high-quality training to build skills in management, business, and leadership.

I gained administrative responsibilities in a variety of roles in the region over time, becoming the head of population health for the market. At the time, we had about 1,000 providers in the Mid-Atlantic Permanente medical group spread across Maryland, Virginia, and the District of Columbia.

While I didn't know every clinician personally, there were only a couple of degrees of separation between those who knew me from my clinical work and those who had met me when I wore an administrator hat. The front-line docs directly caring for patients have more inherent trust in the former than the latter.

All that changed when I went to the Kaiser Permanente main office in Oakland, California. The Permanente physicians from California, Colorado, Hawaii, Georgia, Washington, and Oregon didn't know my name, much less who I was nor how I practiced medicine. I was now one of "them": someone who pushed paper from an ivory tower. My peers knew of me, but had not worked closely with me, and the team that worked for me was being cautious, unsure what to expect.

I moved across the country to work with this completely new group of people, away from my comfort zone and support structure. The challenge came in not knowing what to do next. I had always worked on building strong relationships and driving change with data. In my new role, I had neither, and had to somehow sort out both.

What made that first year so difficult is that I did not realize the threat people in the regions, those closest to the work, can feel from a central office. And at that time, data were still collected locally, and regions wanted to own their own analytics. Approaching the role focused on my own ideas and priorities, and asking regions to bring together their data that they held dear, was like trying to push molasses up a hill: I got nowhere. I was an ineffective leader unable to drive any change.

Around the same time, our boss, Dr. Jack Cochran, invited the entire leadership team to an offsite professional development training. In preparation, we all did work-style assessments of ourselves and of our peers to see how much self-awareness and authenticity we had at work.

In my first 17 years on the job (while working in a variety of regional roles), my self-assessment and others' assessments of me always matched on similar tools; I saw myself the same way I showed up to others. In this new role, with me trying to please people I didn't know, drive change I knew we needed but without a group of aligned colleagues alongside, it was completely the opposite. I had made the fatal mistakes of telling, not asking. Driving, not channeling. Acting, not listening. The mismatch was a real wakeup call. To be a successful system level leader, I needed to start over.

THREE KEYS TO LEADING A HEALTHCARE SYSTEM

I made three key resolutions at that offsite meeting that have helped define my career since, successfully navigating the challenges of leading large healthcare systems:

1. Manage myself first.

In that first year as a system leader, I solicited a lot of feedback on our priorities and how I could accelerate progress. Part of my challenge was that the cacophony of voices felt overwhelming; five executives could have 10 opinions. So to "make everyone happy," I tried to do as much as possible, ending up scattered and feeling like I had to choose between camps. I was constantly stressed, overwhelmed with complexity. I was in react mode vs. lead mode.

I realized the problem was me; I needed to spend more time listening, finding the underlying heart of what we needed to solve, something we could all live with. But to do so, I needed the courage to focus on the *important* over the *urgent*. I needed to say, "Tell me more," "Why is that," "What would that do for our patients," and "How might we do that" regularly. I needed to stop scurrying and get calm.

It's a lesson that I still heed today: the crazier life gets, the calmer I need to be. Deep breaths when passions run high, daily exercise to balance emotions, and regular vacations to recharge resilience are all part of making it through our challenging careers. When a senior leader comes across as harried, brusk, or dismissive, it sabotages the organizational culture. If I want my organization to be calm, focused, and resilient, I need to be calm, focused, and resilient. Taking time for myself is not being selfish, it's part of being a good leader.

2. Empower the team.

In a regional role, one person can be a hero. Great ideas almost always start with one or two strong leaders who motivate others to follow, and the breakthrough spreads. At a system level, it's hard to make an impact with a hero mentality. Humility is much more important than heroism; sorting out how to make the people who work with and for you ever more effective is a force multiplier.

Regular team strategy sessions to determine the path, with huddles to track progress and individual meetings to support varying initiatives is key. And most important? Let them do their work and get the credit. I use simple tactics to live this daily. If I'm cc'd on an email, I don't answer it; I let the team sort it out and only chime in if I'm asked. I trust them to do their work, celebrate the successes and help cushion the blow from any well-thought-through valiant attempts that didn't work.

If there is a problem performer on the team, they are the first to know what needs to be done to fix an issue; if they cannot, they need to move on. Having the right people on the bus is essential at a system level where you're trying to make a broad impact across an organization. When you have that right team, let them fly.

Tight/Loose/Tight Management

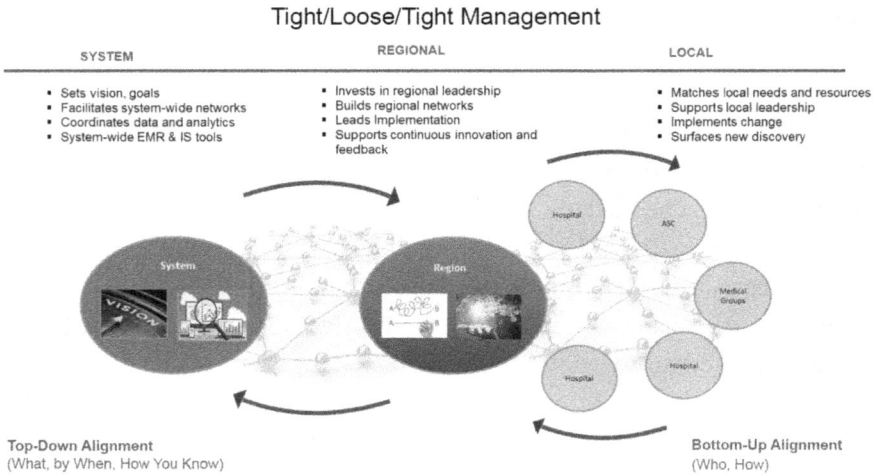

SYSTEM	REGIONAL	LOCAL
• Sets vision, goals • Facilitates system-wide networks • Coordinates data and analytics • System-wide EMR & IS tools	• Invests in regional leadership • Builds regional networks • Leads Implementation • Supports continuous innovation and feedback	• Matches local needs and resources • Supports local leadership • Implements change • Surfaces new discovery

Top-Down Alignment
(What, by When, How You Know)

Bottom-Up Alignment
(Who, How)

FIGURE 1.

3. Listen, synthesize, clarify, prioritize.

I listened to many voices in that first year; unfortunately, I didn't put the pieces together. With deep listening, it's possible to tease out underlying themes of a few foundational issues. Translating what a broad swath of people say into insights that resonate is essential at a system level.

Chief medical officers ensure patients receive the best possible care and health outcomes. The essence of the role is to ensure the organization has the right clinicians with the right tools and skills to make this happen. But much of that happens at the local or regional level. Deciding what specialty mix is needed, where complex surgical care will be offered, or even if evening and weekend office hours should be available are decisions based on local needs in different communities.

A system CMO can align on a few key priorities that improve outcomes for patients, but regions and local leadership need to work out the details based on the local context. I am a firm believer in the tight/loose/tight management system (Figure 1):

- Tight: System sets the critical few clinical priorities for the organization; **What by When.**
- Loose: The regional and local leadership decides **Who** works on the priorities, and **How** they get it done. Learning collaboratives across the regions share what's working (or not).

- Tight: **How You Know**. The system measures the outcomes and critical few process measures to enable learning from the regional variation in processes.

The tight/loose/tight management model helps a system CMO be significantly more effective. Coalescing on a critical few priorities, establishing a way for regions and local divisions to take ownership of implementation while asking them to share how they are doing so, and comparing outcomes to enable a view of what is not only accelerates performance, but ensures the people doing the work buy into the need and value of the work.

Managing myself first, empowering the team, and rigorous prioritization with tight/loose/tight execution was the essential trifecta for me to be effective (after my first failure of a year) in leading large-scale change.

INNOVATING AT SCALE

While my three management rules to be an effective CMO have served me well, they were not the only lessons I learned about being an effective system-level leader.

In today's rapidly shifting environment where knowledge doubles at a blistering pace, new technology is launched daily, and AI has completely changed the game, being able to adopt and embed breakthrough innovations is an essential skill set. A clinical leader can get stuck chasing squirrels – bright, shiny objects that cost time and money to implement and do not live up to the promise of simplifying life for clinicians or patients. To avoid the trap so many organizations and leaders fall into, I decided to base my approach to scaling breakthrough ideas on what worked.

Back in my Kaiser Permanente role, we had some leaders who developed and led breakthrough innovations in safety, quality, and experience that started in one location and then spread like wildfire across the system. Other innovations on the surface seemed equally compelling, but never spread past the unit or office where they'd been developed — a pilot doomed to chug along without making headway.

To understand the recipe for implementing innovation at scale, I brought together a group of individuals who were effective at making change happen. The group included amazing leaders like Dr. Michael Kanter, the physician who developed effective, reliable systems for Complete Care (ensuring care gaps were addressed by the care team) and SureNet (so abnormal lab results were not lost in the cracks of an overly complex EMR). And Dr. Alán Whippy, who recognized in the early 2010s that early identification and treatment of sepsis would have a dramatic impact, making a significant dent in the number one killer of inpatients. And Dr. Jo Carol Hiatt, who recognized that when clinicians stand together to identify and contract for medical devices based on effectiveness, we provide a counterbalance to the outsize profits across the industry, helping keep care affordable for the patients we serve.

Our group was hosted at IDEO, a human-centered design consultancy based in San Francisco. In just a day, by helping the leaders in the room articulate how they had been able to not only develop an idea but scale it across 23,000 physicians and the staff that work with them, we developed a simple proposed model (Figure 2).

I was recruited to Providence before testing this at KP, but was able to put it into action in my new system, supplementing it with the final step (required in a fee-for-service system, less essential in the value based KP environment):

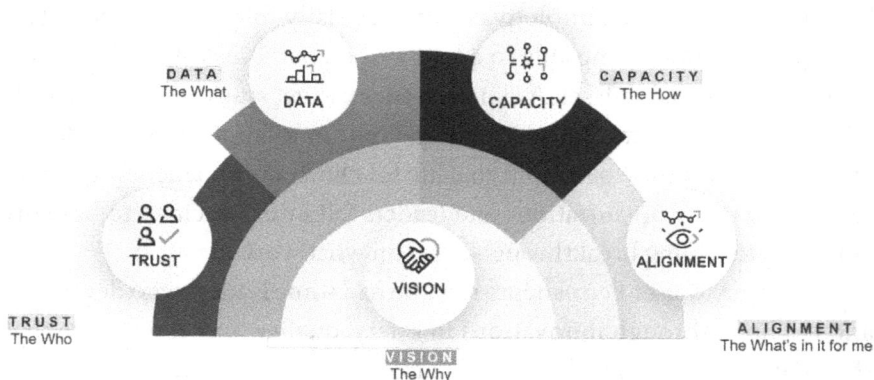

FIGURE 2. Proposed Model

1. **Vision**: Start with why. "We're preventing needless deaths from sepsis," not "We're measuring adherence to a sepsis bundle." (If you have not seen Simon Sinek's TED talk on the topic, it's worth watching: https://youtu.be/u4ZoJKF_VuA?si=AssSB5UbJ9salTJo)

2. **Trust:** Decide on who. Ensure that the leadership team includes trusted leaders with both content knowledge and a following by the people who will be implementing a change. As leadership author Jim Collins puts it: get the right people on the bus. Typically, implementing these initiatives is not a full-time job, but rather another duty as assigned in a day job, so choose people who are effective at teaming to participate in implementing innovative change.

3. **Data:** Focus on data that drive change. Decide on and develop process and outcome measures to be used across the system to determine if any change is an improvement. Deaths from sepsis is a measure that drives change; observed-to-expected ratios for sepsis deaths are not. O/E is not intuitive, it takes statistical understanding to recognize what good looks like. Decreasing the number of people who died from sepsis makes sense to everyone in the organization. And process measures including clinical acknowledgment of a risk score, use of a standardized order set, and adherence to a bundle will move more quickly than an outcome measure like overall deaths. Both measure types are key to rapid progress.

4. **Capacity:** Ensure the skills, tools, and learning networks are supported to operationalize change. Build people's skills in process improvement or lean to boost efficacy. Invest in tools such as standard order sets and/or portable ultrasounds in ICUs to facilitate rapid central line placement. Establish learning networks to ensure when one location figures out a solution to a conundrum others face, their knowledge spreads rapidly.

5. **Alignment:** Ideally, structure incentives to support implementing an innovation, but at a minimum to not disincentivize a change. A real-life example: We had a stated goal in our strategic plan to increase our patients in value-based care (VBC) contracts but most of our physicians' compensation was based on productivity. Paying physicians via RVUs misaligns incentives: To be successful in VBC plans, physicians ideally provide excellent preventive care without requiring an office visit, but a physician who is paid based on RVUs is incentivized to bring them into the office. As a result, clinicians feel told to do one thing but are rewarded for doing the opposite. They get stuck, demoralized, and feel like they can't win.

By applying this model over time to the select few top priorities, at Providence we were able to reduce patients harmed by hospital-acquired infections, reduce deaths from sepsis, enhance healthcare value (improving outcomes at lower cost), and get ever better at driving patient-centered, goal-oriented care.

KEY TAKE HOME LESSONS

In summary, my key take home lessons in being a system CMO are:

1. It's not the same skill set as being a regional CMO; **be ready to learn fast** in moving from one role to the next.

2. Ensure you **spend time on deep listening and self-reflection** when stepping into the larger role. While my mantra of managing myself first, empowering my team, and listening, clarifying, synthesizing, and prioritizing worked for me, it's most important that you develop a systematic approach.

   Determine what you want to achieve in the role, what the organization needs you to achieve, and prioritize the overlap. Large healthcare organizations are like armadas; one boat moving out of line can cause chain reaction disasters or shift the direction of the fleet. Decide how you can do more of the latter and less of the former.

3. Realize that **simplicity and clarity are your friends**. A few big moves, with simple, impactful improvements, will win out over a laundry list of tactics any time.

4. Most importantly, **enjoy the ride**. Few people have the opportunity to make such a significant impact on the lives of so many. Being a system CMO is hard work, but an honor and privilege. Remind yourself daily, smile, and get back to work.

PART V

As a New CMO

CHAPTER 14

The First 90 Days as a CMO

Douglas A. Koekkoek, MD

CONGRATULATIONS, YOU HAVE JUST LANDED your first CMO job. Now the real work begins. A good start will pay dividends for the entire time you are in the role, so getting out of the gate strong should be a priority. Thus, the idea of the *first 90 days plan*.

You will never again get a "first 90 days" for this job, so plan for it and make it count. During these first few months on the job, you aren't expected to know everything or everybody — that is a luxury you won't be afforded six months into the job. The first three months are a time when it is okay to ask dumb questions, or better said, to use "humble inquiry" to ask the probing questions in a way that folks won't become defensive or try to cover their tracks. You will earn respect if you take the time to ask good, thoughtful questions.

This is also the only opportunity you get to make a first impression. First impressions matter and you will be given future latitude and trust if that first impression is favorable. So come prepared. Before you meet people for the first time, know something about them and their work. Look at their past performance appraisals if you have access to them. Check out their LinkedIn profile. Know something about their departments and their committees and ask relevant questions. Be on time and dress appropriately. While you may need to give folks your background so they can get to know you, your first meetings should not be about you — it is about them.

Don't overcommit in these first meetings. You are not expected to have a plan, just a plan to get a plan. Be transparent with the organization about who you will be meeting with and use that feedback to create a more comprehensive plan for how you will prioritize your time and resources in the coming year. I predict you will find individuals jockeying to get time on your calendar to be part of the process.

Make sure folks know your intent is to do a thorough job of learning about the company and its people. You want to understand the problems and priorities of the organization. Use this time to learn the gaps and needs of the organization. Learning the capabilities and resources of the organization is a key objective, and you can't do that without meeting with individuals and assessing the talent. And only after all that learning and listening, do you get to reflect back to them your plan for one more round of feedback. Throughout this process you can also develop consensus and expectations around what they will see you spend your time on.

So that is the main point: The first 90 days is the time to discover the gaps, priorities, and resources available to create a plan, it is not the time in which you accomplish everything, fill every gap, or solve every problem. Sure, there might be some quick wins where you come with prior experience or an idea that folks want to run with that will be successful. Look for those opportunities; they can build confidence and faith in your selection as the right choice. But this is a marathon, not a sprint. Don't miss this chance to listen and put together an assessment.

YOUR STAKEHOLDERS

So, who are those stakeholders you need to meet with in the first 90 days? Some of these individuals will be obvious, others may not be so obvious.

Your Boss

Let's start with your boss, who is likely either the chief executive or, if you are joining a system, the system CMO. You probably already asked this individual many questions in the interview process about what their expectations are for the CMO, what their priorities are for the CMO, and what success for the CMO looks like in the first year. Now it is time to get much more granular.

Ask them what priorities and performance expectations they are being held to by their system leadership or their board of directors and which of those items do they see as being things you will help them achieve. If they have key priorities like CMS 5-star ratings, Hospital Acquired Conditions or Readmission penalty reductions, over what timeline do they expect improvement? This may take some negotiating.

Many hospital administrators have only a vague understanding of the dates included in CMS performance periods that go into these rankings or financial penalties. If they are looking for specific initiatives to improve physician engagement or patient experience, make sure you understand by when, what's been done before, and what resources are available.

Similarly, CMOs are frequently asked to make improvements in safety programs that will reduce the financial liability for malpractice cases. Here, you should ask what is in the cue and when the risk team is expecting to decide on litigation or settlement, and what has been set aside in reserves ... all important questions.

This would be a good time to get clarity on physician contracts. Most hospitals have exclusive call agreements with physician groups, coverage agreements for specialized physician services such as diagnostic imaging, pathology, or standard clinical services like critical care and emergency department staffing. What role does your chief executive intend for you to take in these negotiations? Do they want you to be the primary manager of those relationships and performance metrics or will the chief executive or chief operating officer be the owner of this body of work?

This is obviously just a starter list for those first few meetings with your new boss, but this is the key stakeholder for you to have clear communications with on organizational background and future expectations.

CNO and Medical Staff Leader

Your chief nursing officer and the hospital's elected medical staff leader (president of the medical staff or chief of staff) are also key stakeholders. But these individuals will be your peers and partners, not your bosses. So, while you will want to learn what is important to them, you will find their accountabilities are not necessarily yours.

This is an important dance in which you find common and aligned priorities and areas where you can help each other. Discussing with them what your chief executive is holding you accountable for will likely help them see beyond their responsibilities, and hearing their priorities will do the same for you. Devote time to nurturing these relationships. These individuals will become your friends, colleagues, and sounding boards. You will be more successful if there is a true partnership between you.

Medical Executive Committee Members

Get to know your Medical Executive Committee members individually, not just collectively in the MEC meeting. Know their clinical expertise, know their path to department chair, and any aspirations they may have for future leadership roles.

Two key individuals here are your credentials chair and your peer review chair. Having effective leaders in these roles can make your tenure as CMO so much more effective and manageable. If you have an effective credentialing process that takes seriously the work of keeping unqualified and disruptive physicians off your medical staff membership, you will deal with far fewer performance improvement plans. If you have a peer review process that seeks to not just restrict privileges of incompetent physicians but will work to share important clinical learnings across the organization and encourage voluntary skill and practice enhancements, you will be much more effective at advancing quality and safety in your hospital.

So, get to know these individuals. How experienced are they? Are they willing to take the time needed to do a good job in these roles or do they need further education or mentoring to be effective? Some investment here will pay dividends for years.

Your Circle of Leaders

Who will be in your circle of invested physician leaders who will help you be successful? This is your clinical cabinet. It may include some elected physician leaders, some contracted medical directors, and some leaders from your employed physician medical group. Find these candidates and meet with them as key stakeholders. Invite them into your vision and get them excited about the opportunities to advance the care model and performance of your hospital.

Just like you had partners you trusted and worked closely with in your clinical practice, this small circle of physician leaders will be people you can rely on to get the work done. Again, invest in these conversations, get to know these individuals' clinical expertise, leadership experience and aspirations, and get to know them personally. This is your brain trust and represents the ability to move from individual contributor to a leader of contributors.

Medical Office Staff Director

You will likely have a director or manager of your medical staff office. This key individual knows all the current physician performance improvement plans and the history of current and previous MEC leaders, and can help ensure your department meetings are moving in a forward direction.

This individual can point you to the bylaws, credentialing policies, and rules and regulations of the medical staff. Read these documents several times in your first 90 days. You will be surprised how often knowing the details matters and keeps you out of trouble.

Medical Staff Attorney

And while we are in this domain, remember to find out who your medical staff attorney is. Your lawyer for medical staff affairs and physician contracts is a key stakeholder. Once again, learn their history and experience. Ask what they see as areas you as the incoming CMO should focus on. It will likely be a different list than what your chief executive gave you, but an ounce of prevention on this list will keep some significant problems from becoming a priority of your chief executive.

Quality Improvement and Project Management Team

Leaders of your quality improvement team and project managers who focus on performance improvement may or may not report directly to you in the organizational structure. You should have a good sense of how they partnered with the CMO in the past, what their experience is, and how many staff members they have to help you with improvement projects.

These individuals frequently rose through the clinical ranks and have some important insights into where the real opportunities for clinically impactful improvement in the hospital exist. Similarly, understanding your informatics and IT resources is key background information. So much of how we deliver healthcare today care is dependent upon the functioning of the electronic medical record. These individuals will be key to many improvement projects.

The Administrative Assistant

There is one more stakeholder whom you ignore at your own peril: your administrative assistant. Surprisingly, some CMOs think of these professionals as just someone who manages their calendar and reimbursements. Yet, these people have a birds eye view of how the C-suite operates and they know intimate details of interpersonal conflicts and the idiosyncrasies of the people you will be working with. You will be counting on them to set up all the stakeholder appointments, and they will know who you've missed.

Take the time to interview them in the same way you interview a chief of staff or department chair or other leaders on your stakeholder list. If they have been in the organization for a few years, you may be surprised by how much they know and how many potholes they will prevent you from stepping into.

ORGANIZATIONAL DETAILS

People always come first, but after key stakeholders, you still need some factual details of the organization to be successful. What are the key strategic or growth initiatives that the hospital is undertaking, such as building projects, new clinical partnerships, or key service line growth objectives? Who is the local competition and what are the relative strengths and weaknesses that you both possess in the competitive market?

Know your organization's financial performance and know what budget you must work with. Some CMO roles have their own budget, but many times it may be folded into general administrative or quality budgets. It is more difficult to put forward new quality or service line initiatives that will require additional FTEs if you are in a financial turn-around mode. So, understanding the financial situation on a granular level will keep you from appearing tone deaf with the rest of the administrative team.

Know your emergency department and specialty call coverage. Where are you thin? Where is there competition between physician groups? It is always surprising to me how often ill will can develop between practices within a subspecialty, both working in the same hospital and potentially easing each other's call burden. Often just taking the time to hear each practice's goals and needs, and then creating some clear lines of communication will move adversaries back to being colleagues. Spend some time here and you may strengthen practices and the overall culture in a way that prevents the hospital from having to invest in recruiting or call stipends down the road.

What are the current goals and metrics that leaders are held responsible for and are they tied to financial incentives for leaders and staff? The old adage that "you measure what matters" holds true here.

Most healthcare organizations now have a well-defined data and analytics platform that keeps track of performance metrics. Make sure you get access and permission to log in to review the performance dashboards. If your hospital measures and generates monthly reports on mortality, readmissions, and patient satisfaction, and then provides financial incentives to staff on that performance, you can be sure those items need to belong in your long-term plan.

Most hospitals use some type of CMS reporting software that does a good job of collating and displaying performance data. And whether your hospital uses Premier, Truven, or Quantros to aggregate its quality data matters less than whether you understand how the data are entered or validated.

If the only metrics reviewed regularly are productivity, margin, and market share … well that says something important that you shouldn't miss either. And it doesn't mean you can't put forward a new safety initiative if you happen to have joined a financial oriented hospital; it just means it needs a proforma that shows how it will reduce liability costs, reduce length of stay, or decrease medication utilization in a way that makes financial sense to the organization.

There is likely a variance reporting system with trended safety or unusual occurrence outcomes; make sure you can access this variance reporting system and then spend some time looking at recent trends. Understand how this system relates to peer review and risk management systems. These three systems should have important firewalls that protect their separate function and the integrity and discoverability of the information; however, there is an important bridge to a cohesive safety and improvement culture where each has a way of initiating work in the other.

WALK THE HALLS

After you know the people and the organizational details, it is time to walk the halls of your facility. Many hospitals are complex and have been built over years and decades, so the first few times you may need a tour guide. But after the first few weeks, you spend some time roaming the halls and talking with front-line staff on your own. This is critical, because your ability to move difficult initiatives forward will depend on front-line physicians and nurses understanding that you know their work on a granular level, not just from board rooms and spread sheets. These are different conversations than with key stakeholders; shorter, fewer hard questions, but definitely ask individuals what they are proud of in their departments and what they think needs to be improved.

The key here is visibility and appreciation, not grilling folks for poor performance or inspecting them as a Joint Commission surveyor would. Let them know you care and that you appreciate the work they do every day. Take notes, and if you find an answer or solve their problem, circle back with individuals; you will develop an ardent follower if that behavior of circling back is demonstrated over and over.

MAKE THE PLAN

The first 90 days plan is to meet the people and understand the organization well enough to then take a run at crafting a longer plan and priority list for your job. It is a plan to make a plan. Hopefully by now you know the gaps and the talent and resources needed to fix those gaps. Put this down on paper. Organize it into categories: medical staff, safety, quality, experience, caregiver engagement, growth, financial improvements, technology, and IT infrastructure.

In creating this priority list, do a self-assessment. Where are your own experience and passion? I have often said about 80% of a CMO's job is going to be handed to them by the chief executive or the organization. These are the gaps and performance deficiencies that need to be attended to. No argument on this part of the list; it's the job you have taken. Fixing the performance gaps is part of what it means to be a successful chief medical officer.

But you are likely to have some discretion over the other 20%. And here it is very important to look at where your passion is and what gives you personal satisfaction as a leader. For some of us this is advancing patient safety. For other CMOs it is developing a cohesive medical staff that works well together in a way that reduces burnout and improves engagement. Still others may find they enjoy developing service lines, strategic partnerships, or innovating the care model.

The point is, make sure your plan reserves time for the work that lights your fire professionally. If you can't have something in your work plan every week that is of your own design and is something that you feel is professionally important, you will tire of the day-in and day-out routine and won't be able to sustain your work as a chief medical officer. It's the 80-20 rule: 80% of the work will be handed to you, so keep 20% that you feel personally connected to — that is the recipe for longevity in these roles.

After you put together that list of priorities and initiatives that will define your tenure, the next step is to vet it. Vet it with the same key stakeholders you started the exercise with. You must be open to feedback that you missed something or didn't quite hear things accurately. The plan must be sufficiently flexible to take a fair amount of editing in the first round of vetting for it to be meaningful to leadership, physicians, and staff.

Now you have a plan around which to organize your time. Look forward in your calendar and make sure it reflects that the appropriate time is being allocated to the big issues. Are you spending sufficient time on the key priorities the organization has for you, and that you have for the organization? If not, then you need to manage your calendar, time, and resources differently to meet the key needs of the organization.

One last bit of advice when putting together a plan in your first 90 days: Know that any plan can be changed. If the COVID-19 pandemic taught us anything, it is that we each step into our jobs with the humility that when the environment changes, we must change with it. Who knows when the next pandemic, nursing strike, or blood shortage is going to show up? Every CMO plan must live within the unique healthcare market they find themselves in.

So, when the environment changes, so must your plan. But with that one last caveat to set the correct tone, now you know the people and organization, and have the basic list of priorities to work on, so enjoy the ride. Being a chief medical officer is the best job around.

CHAPTER 15

The Importance of Mentorship

Gabriella Sherman, MD, MBA

A MENTOR PLAYS A PIVOTAL ROLE in the development and ongoing success of a chief medical officer. CMOs are tasked with overseeing the complex clinical operations of an organization and thus must be equipped with both a strong clinical background and the acumen and gravitas to lead and cultivate an effective team.

While most CMOs feel comfortable in their clinical practice environment, stepping into a fully administrative role will be a significant change. As a new CMO, you will need to understand organizational culture, navigate a new and potentially challenging physician landscape, build trust with your team and physician colleagues, and learn how to prioritize local and corporate initiatives.

No textbook or course will give you the practical tools to execute effectively and build your organizational identity and professional reputation as a CMO. A mentor can help you navigate this transition with grace and confidence. This chapter explores the critical importance of mentorship for aspiring and current CMOs and provides practical tools to help you identify a mentor and develop a productive mentor-mentee relationship.

The noun *mentor* was first defined in 1616 and originated from the character of Mentor in Homer's *The Odyssey*. For those of us who may benefit from a Greek history refresher, Odysseus, the King of Ithica, entrusted his young son Telemachus to the care of Mentor, his trusted companion, when he left to lead his army. Mentor was charged with keeping the household undisturbed as well as influencing Telemachus to help him achieve his full potential.

Unfortunately, Odysseus put his trust in the wrong man. Mentor failed to keep the household safe. Multiple suitors lusted after Queen Penelope, Telemachus' mother, in Odysseus' absence. The suitors ate their food, killed their animals, and plotted to kill Telemachus in an effort to seize the family estate. Fortunately, Zeus sent Athena who assumed the form of Mentor and offered Telemachus support and guidance in his father's absence. Athena encouraged Telemachus to speak out against Penelope's suitors and arranged a ship to take Telemachus to safety. Their interactions in *The Odyssey* represent one of the earliest forms of mentorship.

The power of mentorship has been studied extensively and it's clear that mentors and mentees benefit from a successful mentorship relationship. In a recent article published by *Forbes*, surveys of more than 3,000 working professionals concluded that 76% of them believe that a mentor is important to professional growth, yet more than 54% do not have a mentor.[1]

While some organizations have structured mentoring pathways, many do not. As such, it is essential that CMOs are equipped with the tools to identify suitable mentors and develop productive mentoring relationships. Mentors support the personal and professional growth of their mentees and have been shown to improve resiliency and reduce burnout.

I recall vividly while I was away at a conference with my CMO, Dr. Paula Verrette, I asked her why she was so invested in my development. She replied with "A mentor sees something in a person that they do not yet see in themselves." Her thoughtful and radically candid approach to mentorship benefited many aspiring physician leaders.

WHAT IS A MENTOR?

In the simplest of terms, a mentor is a trusted advisor — typically a professional with more experience than their mentee and someone who is willing to share their expertise to help the mentee grow personally and/or professionally. A mentor is usually not your direct supervisor and may even be someone from another organization. They want you to succeed and are willing to invest time and personal capital to guide you on your path.

A mentor recognizes your strengths and is candid with you about your opportunities. They have the organizational "know-how" and are willing to share it. They have a vested interest in your success and understand that mentorship is a partnership.

Adam Grant is an organizational psychologist and one of the top-rated professors whom I had the benefit of learning from during my MBA journey at The Wharton School of Business. Grant summarized it best: "Bad mentors see you as building their brand. They take credit for your success. Great mentors see you as a younger version of themselves. They help you follow in their footsteps. Great mentors see your potential to be a better version of yourself. They help you find your path."

I was very fortunate to benefit from having a great mentor and I hope that this chapter will inspire and motivate you to identify a great mentor as you begin your journey to a rewarding career as a chief medical officer.

WHAT IS MENTORING?

A mentor-mentee relationship is built on a foundation of trust, respect, and a mutual willingness to learn and teach. Mentoring is a development process that is meant to advance the mentee personally and professionally. Mentors share knowledge, open their networks, and often help develop the "softer" skills of leadership.

A mentor is a resource who can often provide guidance in a challenging situation, someone who can help you learn the culture of organization and understand what is left unsaid during a meeting. A mentor can help you learn how to read a room and know when to listen and when to speak. There is no textbook, course, or formal degree that can provide the same insight that a willing mentor is able to offer a mentee.

Mentoring is not a replacement for formal development. While you may gain additional expertise in quality or medical staff operations from your mentor, this is not the purpose of mentorship. To be an effective CMO, you must invest in your own professional development.

A mentor may be able to advise you on useful conferences or resources to expand your fund of knowledge in the quality or regulatory landscape. You should not hesitate to ask your mentor for advice if you feel that you have a knowledge gap and would benefit from additional training. In fact, my mentor was key in my decision to pursue an MBA.

Your mentor is not meant to be your educator but can certainly help augment your learning. A mentor is an excellent resource when looking for guidance on how to navigate an organizational challenge, deal with a difficult physician, or become familiar with the unwritten rules when navigating a complex organization.

A mentoring relationship should be structured from the perspective of cadence and accountability. As noted in the subsequent sections, setting regular mentoring meetings is essential for keeping momentum. Life will get busy as a CMO and multiple priorities will inevitably compete for your time. If your mentor is available and you had the time scheduled with them, do not reschedule. Honor the commitment you made to yourself and to your mentor. Use the time to discuss real scenarios that occurred to see if there is an opportunity for you to do something better or differently in the future. Ask your mentor how they may have addressed something similar. If you are looking for professional growth opportunities, ask your mentor how to gain exposure to them and what you may need to improve upon or learn in order to take that next step.

DEFINING THE BENEFITS OF A MENTOR RELATIONSHIP

Before seeking a mentor, complete an honest inventory of self-acknowledged strengths, opportunities, and specific career goals. Mentorship can be successful only if the mentee is their authentic self during the process. Spend the time understanding your own why before soliciting the help of a potential mentor.

Many find that this exercise is valuable in more ways than just helping in your mentorship journey. Carving out dedicated self-exploration time is essential as you build your professional identity. As an executive leadership coach, I spend time with my clients exploring these topics which have the potential to transform their leadership journey if they are honest with themselves in the process.

The following five questions can serve as a roadmap. Consider writing out your responses, as you may be surprised by the power of honesty in this exercise.

1. **What are my strengths?**
   - Am I confident leading others? Why or why not?
   - Do I have a strategic mindset?
   - How comfortable am I with operationalizing a project?
   - What is the depth and breadth of my expertise in quality, performance improvement, and medical staff?

2. **What are the functional skills that I need to develop?**
   - Have I managed a challenging physician in partnership with a medical executive committee? What about with legal counsel?
   - How comfortable am I with clinical and operational data analysis?
   - Do I feel confident managing, mentoring and coaching other physicians into leadership roles?
   - How comfortable am I with typical managerial functions — hiring, coaching for improvement, terminations?
   - What is my expertise in quality, regulatory and medical staff operations?
3. **What do I enjoy?**
   - What brings meaning to my day?
   - What brings joy to my day?
   - What is my personal leadership philosophy?
4. **Where do I want to be in One year? Three years? Five years?**
   - Short term: What does success as a CMO look like to me?
   - Near term: Do I aspire for local and regional growth opportunities?
   - Long term: Do I plan to continue in the CMO track or pivot?
5. **What are my personal and professional definitions of success?** This was my mentor's favorite question to ask. It is likely that your personal and professional definitions of success will change over time. Be specific here. This is a much more challenging question to answer than you realize.
   - What does success look like for me?
   - How are my definitions of success similar?

CLARIFYING WHAT YOU ARE LOOKING FOR

Behind every great leader is a team of people who helped them succeed. Many executive leaders point to a mentor, a coach, a sponsor, or even all three who helped them navigate unchartered territory.

Important career decisions are often made in a room where you are not present. While you may in fact be the best candidate, the most talented, hardest working leader within an organization, there may come a time when that does not inevitably translate to a promotion. Having a sponsor in the room where the decision is being made can contribute positively to your success within many organizations.

A sponsor is someone who will vouch for you, for your professional skill set, your attitude, your thoughtfulness, and use their currency on your behalf. They have a personal stake in your success. Look for those individuals who have a seat at the table when important decisions are being made. Build a relationship, share your why, and be direct in your ask of how they can help you on your journey.

A coach has a very different role than a mentor or a sponsor. They can be helpful at any point in your career, as the most seasoned and talented leaders benefit from ongoing coaching.

A coach is a trained professional who can help you examine a situation through a different lens. They can serve as a neutral sounding board to help you reframe your thoughts and partner with you to set and achieve goals that are meaningful to you. Organizations often offer executive leadership coaching for new leaders. Ask your leader or HR team about potential opportunities for coaching through your company.

Many new C-suite leaders use the terms mentor, coach and sponsor interchangeably. However, the respective roles serve quite different functions and it is essential that as a CMO you are aware of the differences so that you can solicit the right type of development pathway to optimize your personal and professional success.

HOW TO FIND A MENTOR

On your journey, you will meet many individuals who hold executive roles and have great influence within an organization but may not embody your vision of leadership. It is unlikely that these individuals will add value to you by serving you as a mentor.

Look for someone who has held a similar role to the one you currently hold or aspire to have as a next step in your professional journey. Identify someone who has a passion for sharing stories and, most importantly, who seems trustworthy.

While it may be easy to reach out to your regional CMO and ask them to be a mentor, consider finding someone who is not in your reporting structure. Your manager has a duty to fulfill the requirements of the organization and your personal and professional development may not be their top priority. It may also be challenging to be vulnerable and authentic with your manager, depending on the culture of the organization.

If you are joining a new health system, consider finding a seasoned CMO within the system. They can provide practical institutional knowledge that may be hard to decode as a new executive. Other options may include identifying another C-suite leader such as a chief nursing officer or chief operating officer. Check with your human resources team to see if the organization has a structured mentorship program to connect you with a suitable mentor.

You may consider networking outside of your organization through platforms like LinkedIn or Doximity. Start by identifying individuals with the appropriate title who share a mutual connection with you. Before reaching out to them directly, check with your connection to see if this is someone whom they believe would be willing and able to serve as a mentor to you.

MAKING THE ASK

Asking someone to be your mentor involves a thoughtful and respectful approach. Be considerate of their time by learning more about your potential mentor's background in advance of the discussion. Come prepared, as you will set the tone for the possibility of a future relationship.

Do your homework in advance of the meeting.
- What roles has this individual held?
- What is their educational background?
- How long have they been with their organization(s)?

Identify the reasons you believe this individual would serve as a great mentor.
- What specific skills can this mentor help me develop?
- What other individuals are within this person's network who may be a mutually beneficial contact?
- What can I offer this mentor as part of our relationship?

Once you are able to clearly articulate the above, synthesize your ask and reach out to your potential mentor(s). Ask for some time to meet with them in-person, if possible. Identify a location that is low-key and convenient for your mentor. Engage them in an informal way to build rapport and gauge compatibility.

Be clear and concise in your ask of why you are looking for a mentor. Why do you believe they may be a good fit, and what specifically are you hoping to accomplish by partnering with them? Be prepared for the possibility that they may decline due to time constraints or other commitments. If they decline, express gratitude for their time and remain open to future interactions or advice.

If they agree, thank them and follow-up with a thank you over email. Identify the appropriate time frame for your next meeting and set it up. It is important to note, that while we spent part of this chapter discussing how to make the ask, more than 60% of mentor relationships develop naturally without any formal ask.[1] Thus, always place value on relationship building, as many mentorships evolve in an informal environment.

YOUR FIRST MEETING

The most important part of a mentoring relationship is a concerted effort by the mentee to build a relationship with the mentor. Your mentor is giving you the gift of time and you should honor that by making the best use of your time together.

1. **Set the tone by cultivating a foundation for a trusting relationship.** Share more about your background. Share your self-identified strengths and areas of opportunity. Allow your mentor to have an opportunity to share more about themselves and their ambitions. Get to know them as a person, not just an employee with a title in the organization.

2. **Set expectations with your mentor.** Remind them what you hope to learn and gain from the mentoring relationship and ask them what they expect of you in the process. Set the ground rules for your engagement (i.e., candor, confidentiality, authenticity, follow-up frequency).

3. **See if there is an opportunity for you to help your mentor in the process, as the best mentoring relationships add value to both parties.** As a mentee, be thoughtful of trying to create a symbiotic relationship. Is there a project you can take the lead on that can provide value to your mentor? Is there an opportunity to recognize your mentor within the organization for their time and commitment? Is there someone within your network who may benefit your mentor through an introduction? More on this topic in the section on reverse mentoring.

Always end the conversation with an action plan that you are going to work on in advance of your next meeting. This will keep you accountable to yourself and your mentor in the process.

A STRUCTURED ACCOUNTABILITY PROCESS

Consider creating a documented mentoring plan that you can use as a reference throughout the mentorship relationship. This is an accountability plan for you, not your mentor. Mentorship has the power to transform your personal and professional trajectory if you are willing to take a risk. This may mean getting out of your comfort zone as a leader by taking on a new project, challenging the status quo, or learning to listen for understanding and not for framing a response.

Keep notes of what you worked on between mentoring sessions and consider following up with your mentor to share the progress you are making. Your mentor will certainly appreciate that their time has been well spent. Remember, your mentor may become a sponsor or help recruit a sponsor for you. Genuine gratitude is always appreciated and true leaders find that developing others brings great meaning to their lives.

WHAT ABOUT REVERSE MENTORING?

"Mentoring is not a transfer of wisdom from one to another. It's a relationship where two people grow together."[2]) Great mentors are also passionate learners. As discussed earlier, a mentorship relationship is built on trust, authenticity, and vulnerability. As a mentee you have the opportunity to share insights that will help a mentor and an organization grow.

Reverse mentoring occurs when a mentee is able to provide insights to a more senior mentor on various topics of strategic and cultural relevance. The benefits of reverse mentoring have been well described in the literature and are an opportunity for progressive organizations to recognize the value of a well-defined mentorship program. The four main benefits of reverse mentoring noted by Jordan and Sorell in their Harvard Business Review article[3] are:

1. **Increased retention of millennials:** Senior executives have learned about the value and importance of establishing connections and demonstrating appreciation for their teams.

2. **Sharing of digital skills:** Mentees are often younger and more adept at social media and technology. Considering the profound impact of artificial intelligence and digital transformation, healthcare organizations and mentors have the potential to benefit tremendously from their more tech savvy mentees.

3. **Driving cultural change:** Reverse mentoring has been shown to help senior executives understand what is important to their teams. I recall one of the keynote speakers at the Institute of Healthcare Improvement who referenced changing the conversation from "What's the matter?" to "What matters to you?" Getting to the heart of what matters to team members and fellow colleagues allows for necessary culture change.

4. **Promoting diversity:** Diverse viewpoints are essential to advancing healthcare into the future. Reverse mentoring gives credibility to diverse voices in the room and can help mentees get a seat at the proverbial table. We need the diversity of thought, the diversity of talent, and the diversity of people to propel our organizations forward.

As a mentee, look for opportunities for reverse mentorship with your mentor. Furthermore, as you progress in your career, you will find opportunities to mentor others. I hope that you will embrace the chance to help someone else on their journey and find personal and professional satisfaction in the process.

THE TOP FIVE LESSONS I LEARNED FROM MY MENTOR

1. **Get to know people as people:** Fundamentally, we are all human. Whether you have fellow physicians on your team or non-clinical administrators, we all have a desire to be known and add value. Find out what is important to others and build intentional relationships. When your colleagues feel understood, they become less defensive and open to feedback. Your relationships will carry you further than you may realize in your role as a CMO.

2. **Never eat lunch alone:** I have walked past many administrative offices at lunch and witness leaders eating alone at their desk. While we all have competing priorities, take the 15-30 minutes to intentionally

engage with others over a meal. I have learned more about why quality initiatives succeed or fail in the doctor's dining room than in most formal meetings.

3. **If you sit quietly and listen, people will tell you everything you need to know.** I used to joke that my CMO's office was a cross between a therapy room and a confessional. At the time, I didn't understand why others divulged so much information. However, as I progressed on my own journey, I appreciated the value of being an active listener and listening to understand not to speak.

4. **You can be right, or you can be successful.** As a CMO, your goal is not to be right and to prove your point. Your goal is to foster clinical and operational excellence through your leadership and influence. Focus on the end goal of success, not on proving a point.

5. **Just be excellent.** In everything that you do, focus on excellence. Bring your best to every situation and know that you are in the role because you have the expertise and organizational trust to do the work. Find others who will help you and mentor you on your journey to excellence.

Chief medical officers provide tremendous value to organizations by creating environments that foster collaboration in an effort to deliver clinical and operational excellence. Historically, the journey to the C-suite for physicians has been through the medical staff ranks with chairmanships and directorships. While those skills have tremendous value, the CMO of today is truly a strategic partner to the C-suite. The role is no longer simply focused on quality and medical staff but has transcended into the business and clinical operations realm. All CMOs can benefit from mentors who can provide them guidance and help them navigate the complexities of today's healthcare landscape.

REFERENCES

1. Comaford C. 76% of People Think Mentors Are Important, But Only 37% Have One. Forbes. July 3, 2019.
2. Grant A. The Three Big Myths of Mentoring. TED Podcast. October 17, 2023.
3. Jordan J, Sorell M. Why Reverse Mentoring Works and How to Do It Right. Harvard Business Review. October 3, 2019.

Contributors

Michele L. Arnold, MD, MBA
Vice President/Chief Medical Officer
Intermountain Health St. Mary's Regional Hospital
Grand Junction, CO

Steven D. Brass, MD, MPH, MBA, FACHE
Executive Vice President, Chief Medical Executive
Harris Health System
Houston, TX

Amy L. Compton-Phillips, MD
President, Chief Physician Executive
Press Ganey
Seattle, WA

Reka Danko, MD
Chief Medical Officer
Saint Mary's Regional Medical Center
Reno, NV

Gary A. Foster
Healthcare Career Transition Coach
Turning Point Career Services
Highland Ranch, CO

Christopher P. Hall, MD, MBA
Chief Quality and Patient Safety Officer
PeaceHealth
Brush Prairie, WA

Rex Hoffman, MD, MBA, FACHE, CPE
Chief Medical Officer and Executive Director of Operations
Providence Holy Cross Medical Center
Mission Hills, CA

Douglas A. Koekkoek, MD
Chief Physician and Clinical Executive
PeaceHealth
Happy Valley, OR

Michael J. Menen, MD
Chief Medical Officer
MedReview
Glen Allen, VA

Mark D. Olszyk, MD, MBA, CPE, FACEP, FACHE, FAAPL, FFSMB
Chief Medical Officer
Carroll Hospital
Westminster, MD

Lee S. Scheinbart, MD, CPE
Chief Health Affairs Officer
Burrell College of Osteopathic Medicine
Melbourne, FL

Gabriella Sherman, MD, MBA
Chief Medical Officer
HCA Los Robles Health System
Thousand Oaks, CA

www.ingramcontent.com/pod-product-compliance
Lightning Source LLC
Chambersburg PA
CBHW070719220326
41598CB00024BA/3224